T0342394

Machine Learning in Asset Pricing

Princeton Lectures in Finance
Markus K. Brunnermeier, *Series Editor*

The Princeton Lectures in Finance, published by arrangement with the Bendheim Center for Finance of Princeton University, are based on annual lectures offered at Princeton University. Each year, the Bendheim Center invites a leading figure in the field of finance to deliver a set of lectures on a topic of major significance to researchers and professionals around the world.

Stephen A. Ross, *Neoclassical Finance*

William F. Sharpe, *Investors and Markets: Portfolio Choices, Asset Prices, and Investment Advice*

Darrell Duffie, *Dark Markets: Asset Pricing and Information Transmission in Over-the-Counter Markets*

Stefan Nagel, *Machine Learning in Asset Pricing*

Machine Learning in Asset Pricing

Stefan Nagel

PRINCETON UNIVERSITY PRESS

PRINCETON AND OXFORD

Requests for permission to reproduce material from this work should be sent to permissions@press.princeton.edu

Published by Princeton University Press
41 William Street, Princeton, New Jersey 08540
6 Oxford Street, Woodstock, Oxfordshire OX20 1TR

press.princeton.edu

All Rights Reserved

ISBN 978-0-691-218700
ISBN (e-book) 978-0-691-218717

British Library Cataloging-in-Publication Data is available

Editorial: Joe Jackson and Jacqueline Delaney
Production Editorial: Brigitte Pelner
Jacket Design: Karl Spurzem
Production: Erin Suydam
Publicity: Kate Hensley (US) and Kathryn Stevens (UK)

This book has been composed in Sabon

Printed on acid-free paper ∞

Printed in the United States of America

1 3 5 7 9 10 8 6 4 2

To Ksenija and Marko

_____

CONTENTS

PREFACE

THIS BOOK IS an expanded version of the *Princeton Lectures in Finance* that I gave at Princeton University in May 2019. I am grateful to Markus Brunnermeier and the Bendheim Center for Finance at Princeton University for their hospitality. I also thank Princeton University Press and its economics editor, Joe Jackson, for supporting this book project. It gave me a great opportunity to reflect on the recent progress of machine learning in asset pricing and the open questions that research could tackle in the future.

My interest in machine learning applications in asset pricing grew out of joint projects with my co-authors Serhiy Kozak and Shrihari Santosh that we started when Serhiy and I were colleagues at the University of Michigan. Looking at the academic literature on stock returns, one of our areas of interest, we saw a challenge that called for a new approach. At the time, research on the determinants of stock returns was struggling to make sense of the fact that a huge number of different firm characteristics seemed to have a role in predicting differences in future returns between stocks. Yet, published research studies that proposed a new predictor evaluated its predictive performance relative to a sparse selection of only a small number of already-known predictors. This begged the question whether many of the predictors documented in the literature would actually be redundant if evaluated jointly. It also left open the question whether these predictors could have important inter-action effects. A proper characterization of the investment opportunities in equity markets would have to consider a large set of predictors jointly. Machine learning methods were appealing to us as a natural solution for these challenges. One of the papers that resulted from this collaboration (Kozak, Nagel, and Santosh 2020) forms the core of Chapter 4.

More recently, Ian Martin and I started thinking about machine learning methods as a model of belief formation for sophisticated economic agents. For investors, for example, forecasts are crucial decision inputs. Like data scientists applying machine learning techniques to big data sets, investors face an enormous number of potentially relevant predictor variables. To explain the properties of asset prices, it therefore seems important that theoretical models account for the high-dimensional nature of investors' learning problem. Modeling economic agents as machine learners gives them sophisticated tools to deal with this problem in a realistically complex environment. Chapter 5 takes some first steps toward such an asset pricing model. A more extensive exposition of this model is in a joint paper of ours (Martin and Nagel 2019).

I owe a great debt to my co-authors on these projects. Much of what I write about in this book reflects what I have learned in our collaboration. I am also grateful to Ralph Koijen, Ian Martin, Shrihari Santosh, Anirudha Balasubramanian, David Yang, students in my PhD classes at the University of Chicago, and two anonymous reviewers for feedback on drafts of this book. Tianshu Liu and Michael Yip provided excellent research assistance. I am also pleased to acknowledge financial support from the Center for Research in Security Prices (CRSP) at the University of Chicago.

Machine Learning in Asset Pricing

Chapter 1

INTRODUCTION

PREDICTION PROBLEMS ARE central to asset pricing. To price stocks, investors must forecast firms' future cash flows. Investors seeking out-performing trading strategies search for signals that predict asset returns. Researchers testing asset pricing models look for predictor variables that can forecast return differences between assets or that capture forecastable variation in returns across time. Models of credit risk require predictors of default. Hedging and risk management models require forecasts of asset return comovement.

The number of predictor variables that are potentially relevant in these applications is enormous. Technological advances have led to an explo-sive growth in the amount of information that is available to investors and analysts. Even if we look just at the narrow slice of data that can be extracted from corporate financial reports, the growth in data avail-ability has been staggering. Figure 1.1 provides some rough estimates. One hundred years ago, printed annual volumes like the *Moody's* man-uals that summarized corporate financial reports represented much of what was readily available to the public. With the advent of electronic computing, databases like COMPUSTAT expanded coverage to perhaps hundreds or thousands of variables per firm. Today, there is an almost uncountable number of variables that one can construct from publicly available information. The SEC's Edgar database contains financial report data on the order of magnitude of terabytes. With textual analysis, one could probably construct a million variables for each firm from these files.

Corporate financial reports represent only a small fraction of what is potentially available to investors. Databases that record the past history of market prices and transactions contain a gigantic volume of data; sen-timent measures can be extracted from social media; online reviews by customers and employees may contain valuable information; and many other data sources could be relevant.

This abundance of potential predictor variables gives rise to a statis-tical problem. As an example, consider the case of cross-sectional stock return prediction. Say there are $N = 5000$ stocks for which we can observe returns. The number of return predictors, J, that we might consider for forecasting differences in stocks' returns could easily exceed the num-ber of stocks. Is it possible to estimate the relationship between so many

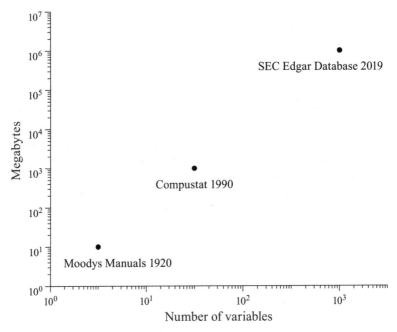

Figure 1.1. Corporate financial reports: 'Big data'

predictors and future returns in a way that delivers useful forecasts of returns?

Conventional statistical techniques like ordinary least squares regression (OLS) are not designed for such high-dimensional settings where J is big relative to N. When $J > N$, OLS regression doesn't have a unique solution. And even if $J < N$, but J is not much smaller than N, the OLS estimator often does not produce useful predictions. With such a high number of explanatory variables, the OLS regression overfits noise. This leads to a good in-sample fit, but poor out-of-sample forecasts.

1.1   AD HOC SPARSITY IN EMPIRICAL ASSET PRICING

Research in asset pricing has, until recently, side-stepped this high-dimensionality problem by focusing on low-dimensional models. Work on cross-sectional stock return prediction, for example, has focused on regressions with a small number of firm characteristics. Collectively, researchers have investigated the predictive power of a large number of firm characteristics, but in any individual study, the number of predictors considered by researchers is typically small. Similarly, researchers looking to summarize the investment opportunities in the cross-section of stock returns with factor models have focused on models with a very small number of factors. For example, Hou, Xue, and Zhang (2015) and Fama and French (2015) include only three or four factors in addition to the value-weighted market portfolio excess return in their factor models. These factors are portfolios constructed based on firm characteristics such as firm size, profitability, investment, or the ratio of the firm's book equity to market equity.

Given the background of an enormously large number of variables that could potentially be relevant for predicting returns and for constructing characteristics-based factor portfolios, focusing on such a small number of factors effectively means that the researchers are imposing a very high degree of *sparsity* on these models. Among the hundreds, thousands, or more potential factors, researchers have chosen a specification that sets the effect of almost all of them to zero.

Imposing such extreme sparsity on the model ensures that conventional statistical methods are well behaved. But the imposition of sparsity is ad hoc. The researchers proposing these models have tested their low-dimensional factor models only against a small subset of the universe of factors that one could potentially construct based on firm-level variables. So we do not really know how much these models miss, in terms of predictive power, relative to the joint effect of this large number of omitted factors. In this regard, it is interesting to note that the number of "standard" factors that researchers view as necessary to adequately capture the cross-section of expected stock returns has been trending up over time. Fama and French (1993) started with three, then came four- and five-factor versions, and Barillas and Shanken (2018) suggest that six are necessary. One interpretation of this expansion in the number of factors is that the literature is slowly adjusting to the fact that there are, indeed, relevant omitted factors.

1.2 Ad hoc Sparsity in Theoretical Asset Pricing

These issues are not only relevant for empirical research in asset pricing, but they also raise questions about theoretical modeling of investor decision making. Asset prices reflect investors' expectations of future asset payoffs. But how do investors come up with these expectations? Real-world investors face the same problem that empirical asset pricing researchers face: there is an enormous number of potentially relevant predictor variables. Distilling them into a good forecasting model is a high-dimensional problem that conventional statistical methods are not well suited for.

Most theoretical asset pricing models assume rational expectations. This assumption is much stronger than just rationality of expectations. In these models, investors do not have to estimate the forecasting model—they already know it. More precisely, investors know perfectly the functional relationship between any relevant predictor variables and the variables they would like to forecast. Given the values of the predictor variables, investors are assumed to be able to calculate the conditional expectations of the forecasted variables. This assumption is often motivated with the idea that the model is meant to represent an equilibrium that would be reached after investors have had time to learn these functional relationships in a stable environment. Even in a low-dimensional setting, the assumption that the learning process has reached an end is questionable. Indeed, Timmermann (1993), Lewellen and Shanken (2002), Collin-Dufresne, Johannes, and Lochstoer (2017), and Nagel and Xu (2019) have argued that investor learning about parameters of the data-generating process is important for understanding asset prices. In a more realistic high-dimensional setting in which investors have to extract the predictive information from thousands of observable variables, the investors-have-already-learned argument is even less convincing.

Arguably, therefore, we should have theoretical models in which investors struggle with high dimensionality in the same way as econometricians do when they study asset price data. Existing models in which investors learn about forecasting models and their parameters typically assume that investors condition their forecasts on a small number of predictors. This sparsity is imposed ad hoc. It seems difficult to make the case that such a sparse representation adequately reflects the forecasting environment faced by real-world investors. Possibly, this mismatch between the difficulty of the prediction problem faced by investors in theoretical models and the difficulty of prediction problems in the real world could be a cause of the empirical shortcomings of existing theoretical asset pricing models.

1.3   Machine Learning

Machine Learning (ML) offers tools to tackle high-dimensional prediction problems. Broadly, ML involves algorithms that allow computers to learn from data. The computer is fed training data to learn, and then the trained algorithm can be used to make predictions. For example, in image recognition, an algorithm could be fed data on image *features* (numerical color values for each image pixel) from a large number of images that are *labeled* into categories. To take an extremely simple case, say we are interested in classifying images of food into ones showing hot dogs and

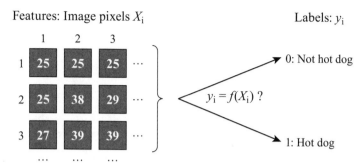

Figure 1.2. Image classification example

ones that do not show hot dogs. From the training data set of already-labeled images, the ML algorithm learns the relationship between image pixels and the classification as a hot dog or not hot dog. Figure 1.2 provides a stylized illustration. Once trained, the algorithm can then be used to predict, for not-yet-classified images, whether they show a hot dog or not a hot dog. In other applications, trained ML algorithms may classify email as spam based on email content, predict tumors based on gene expression data, or interpret sensor data in autonomous driving.

In many of these ML applications, the number of features is extremely large, and often larger than the number of observations that are available to train the algorithm. Conventional statistical tools like ordinary least-squares (OLS) regression would not work in such a setting. Much of the success of ML in practice is due to the development of effective methods to discipline the estimation such that the estimated model (or trained algorithm) produces useful out-of-sample forecasts.

The ML literature therefore offers a rich toolbox to tackle asset pricing prediction problems in high-dimensional settings. Many of these methods are not fundamentally new to the statistics literature, but the ML community has pushed them very successfully into applications. By experimenting heavily and focusing on methods that "work" rather than on understanding the theoretical properties of estimators, the ML literature has assembled an impressive array of methods that have proven to be useful in practical prediction problems. The aim of this book is to survey some of the first steps that asset pricing research has taken to bring these tools into asset pricing, highlight current challenges, and sketch some paths that researchers could take going forward.

The ML toolbox offers the opportunity to analyze asset prices without imposing extreme ad hoc sparsity on prediction problems. In empirical work, ML tools allow an econometrician to take into account the joint effect of a large number of predictor variables. In theoretical

TABLE 1.1
Terminology in ML and Statistics

ML	Statistics
Training, Learning	Estimation
Learner, Algorithm	Model, Estimator
Features	Covariates, Explanatory Variables, Independent Variables, Predictors
Target, Label, Output	Dependent Variable
Example, Instance	Data Point, Observation

work, investors can be modeled as machine learners in a realistic high-dimensional environment.

A recurrent theme throughout this book is that even though ML methods have been impressively successful in a wide variety of applications, using these tools off the shelf in asset pricing is not necessarily going to work well. The properties of data in asset pricing applications are often substantially different from those in technology, medicine, and other scientific fields. Successful application of ML methods in asset pricing therefore will often require some adaptation. To develop appropriate adaptations, we need to bring in some prior economic knowledge about the environment that generates the data. The idea, sometimes associated with ML, that one could make predictions in an entirely data-driven automated fashion is too good to be true. Much of this book is devoted to the question of how we can use economic reasoning to make ML tools effective in asset pricing.

Bayesian statistics offers a framework to incorporate prior knowledge into statistical estimation. The Bayesian framework therefore allows us to build a bridge between economic theories of asset pricing and ML. At various points throughout the book I draw on Bayesian statistics to give an interpretation of ML methods and to suggest economically motivated adaptations of these methods.

1.4 TERMINOLOGY

Coming from computer science, the machine learning literature has developed its own terminology. The concepts and methods often overlap with similar ones in the statistics literature, but they are named differently. This can be confusing. Table 1.1 lists some common terms that will appear throughout various parts of this book. I will use the ML and statistics terminology interchangeably.

1.5 SUPERVISED AND UNSUPERVISED LEARNING

ML methods can be broadly classified into two categories. *Supervised* learning basically refers to regression methods. The training data that is used to train the algorithm comes with features x_i and labels y_i. The goal is to find a function $y_i = f(x_i)$ that maps features into labels. These methods are called supervised learning because one can view the training of the algorithm as a learning process supervised by a "teacher." The learner makes predictions based on x_i in the training data. By revealing the correct labels y_i, the teacher tells the learner whether the prediction was correct. This information about correct or incorrect predictions is used by the learner to tweak the estimate of the function. Once the training is completed, this learned function can then be used to predict labels out-of-sample in data sets where we only have features, but not labels. The image classification example we discussed earlier belongs to this supervised learning category, but there is a large number of other methods that belong into this category as well. Chapter 2 reviews some of the most important ones.

In *unsupervised* learning, the data that is used to train the algorithm only has features, not labels. The goal in unsupervised learning is to find a compressed summary of the data that captures its essential properties. One simple example of a method in this category is principal component analysis (PCA). In PCA, a set of variables is approximated with a smaller number of underlying factors that capture a large amount of the common variation among the variables.

Methods in both categories have useful applications in asset pricing. In this book, I focus largely on supervised learning. One of the fundamental problems in asset pricing—both for financial economists studying asset prices and for investment practitioners—is the estimation of expected asset returns conditional on a set of predictor variables. This is, effectively, a supervised learning problem. Similarly, estimation of cash flow forecasting models in asset valuation is a supervised learning problem. Unsupervised learning methods often play a secondary role in asset pricing applications, for example, in an initial dimension-reduction step that summarizes data before it is fed into a supervised learning algorithm. The distinction between supervised and unsupervised learning in asset pricing applications is not as sharp as it may seem, though. As we will see, some supervised learning approaches effectively have built-in dimension-reduction elements that are similar to those in unsupervised learning approaches.

1.6 Limitations of This Book

This book has some limitations that I would like to clarify at the outset. First, this book is primarily a book about asset pricing. I discuss the application of ML techniques in asset pricing, but this book is not the place to look for information on the latest new developments in ML. Moreover, I do not devote much space to computational questions. This is not because computational issues are unimportant. Quite to the contrary. The success of ML in analyzing huge, high-dimensional data sets is founded on many clever computational advances. But these topics are covered well in the ML literature. Conceptual questions about the suitability of ML tools for asset pricing problems have received comparatively less attention. The focus of this book is on closing this gap.

Second, this book is not an exhaustive survey of machine learning methods in asset pricing. There are many exciting new approaches in current working papers and recently published studies, but I will be able to discuss only a small number of these. Rather than attempting to provide a comprehensive review of the literature, my objective is to highlight the opportunities that exist and the generic challenges that arise when we apply ML methods in asset pricing. The array of available ML tools is vast. I hope to provide some useful thoughts on issues that we need to consider when we bring them into asset pricing. One theme that I return to throughout the book is that economic restrictions are important. To reap the full benefit of ML methods in asset pricing, we need to bring in a limited dose of economic reasoning when we pick from the ML toolbox and make specification choices. Off-the-shelf application of ML techniques without thoughtful adaptation to the specific properties of data in asset pricing is unlikely to work well.

Third, within the area of asset pricing, I focus mostly on cross-sectional return prediction applications. There are certainly other areas in asset pricing where ML methods can be useful, too. For example, valuation models require predictions of asset fundamentals, credit risk models require prediction of credit risk realizations, and risk management applications require predictions of codependencies between asset prices. For all of these, ML techniques can be useful for bringing in high-dimensional predictive information and for handling nonlinear relationships. Yet, a short book like this one necessarily has to be selective. The focus on cross-sectional return prediction in this book simply reflects what I have been working on in my own research. I nevertheless hope that by using these specific applications for illustration, I can provide some insights that generalize beyond these specific settings.

Finally, throughout this book, I often highlight open questions rather than providing definite answers. This book therefore does not offer cookbook recipes for applying ML techniques in asset pricing. Instead, by pointing out interesting unresolved issues, I hope to provide some inspiration for future research that addresses these issues. In this spirit, the last chapter summarizes a number of open research questions that are particularly important for further progress in this area of asset pricing.

1.7 ORGANIZATION OF THIS BOOK

The rest of this book is organized as follows. Chapter 2 provides a brief overview of a number of basic supervised learning methods. The chapter begins by reviewing regression methods that are designed to predict continuous variables, including ridge regression, lasso, trees and random forests, and neural networks. Several of these learning algorithms involve hyperparameters that need to be set in advance, before the actual estimation. Chapter 2 discusses data-driven methods of tuning these hyperparameters to optimize the predictive performance of the learning algorithm. Hyperparameters often control the degree of regularization imposed on the estimation. Chapter 2 ends with a brief illustration of a Bayesian interpretation of regularization. In this interpretation, regularization corresponds to imposing certain prior distributions on model parameters. We use this Bayesian interpretation in subsequent chapters inject economic reasoning and prior knowledge into the design of ML approaches in asset pricing.

Chapter 3 explores challenges that arise when applying ML methods in asset pricing. The chapter starts by outlining some key differences between the properties of data that most ML algorithms have been developed for and the properties of data that are typical in asset pricing. Throughout the chapter, I illustrate some of these issues with a concrete empirical example of cross-sectional stock return prediction using each stock's own price history as source of predictive information. The chapter highlights that while ML methods are well suited for the prediction problems that arise in asset pricing, these techniques require significant adaptation if they are to deliver on their full potential. What works in typical ML applications, say in the technology sector or biostatistics, does not necessarily work well in asset pricing. Among other things, the low signal-to-noise ratio in asset pricing applications means that attempts to simply let the data speak within an extremely flexible framework are unlikely to yield good results. We will have to impose some structure on the learning algorithm. To do so, we need to connect the ML methods to basic economic frameworks of asset pricing and portfolio choice. Some principles from Bayesian statistics are useful for making this connection.

Chapter 4 describes an approach that makes some progress in this direction. It starts from a basic mean-variance portfolio choice problem—or, equivalently, the problem of finding a stochastic discount factor expressed as a linear combination of asset returns—and the notion that near-arbitrage opportunities are unlikely to exist in the stock market. By formulating Bayesian prior beliefs about the risk-return opportunities in the market, this framework allows us to impose economically motivated constraints on the return prediction problem. The estimator that emerges from this approach is similar to the elastic net estimator common in many ML applications, but with some important differences that come from taking into account the fact that prediction error covariances are an important determinant of a portfolio risk-return profile. The empirical application of this estimator uses a broad set of firm characteristics as return predictors, as well as nonlinear transformations of those, including pairwise interactions between characteristics. The empirical findings suggest that imposing economically motivated prior beliefs is important for obtaining good out-of-sample predictive performance.

Chapter 5 takes a theoretical perspective. The earlier chapters show that statistical analysis of financial market data must address the fact that the environment is high-dimensional and ML methods provide a good toolbox for this purpose. But what about the investors whose investment decisions determine the asset prices that feed into these statistical analyses? If the information environment in financial markets is such that the prediction problems are high-dimensional, investors in theoretical models of financial markets should presumably face this high dimensionality, too. Machine learning methods therefore provide an attractive blueprint for modeling investor belief formation in theoretical models. Chapter 5 pursues this approach. To focus on fundamental issues, we consider a simple environment in which investors must learn from historical data the relationship between stocks' cash flows and a large set of firm characteristics that serve as predictor variables. Investors are Bayesian and shrink their prediction model estimates toward objectively correct prior beliefs. In equilibrium, stocks are priced such that returns are unpredictable out-of-sample. However, returns are strongly predictable in-sample in ex-post statistical analyses of returns. This is due to the fact that an econometrician analyzing data ex post with in-sample analyses has the advantage of hindsight knowledge that investors in real time do not have. In a low-dimensional environment this implicit advantage of the econometrician can be small, but it is large in a high-dimensional environment. In-sample regressions are therefore ill suited for inferring risk premia or the effects of behavioral biases of investors from asset price data.

Chapter 6 concludes the book by outlining a research agenda for future research on ML in asset pricing.

Chapter 2

SUPERVISED LEARNING

IN THIS CHAPTER, I provide a brief overview of supervised learning methods. The literature on this topic is vast and rapidly evolving. The overview in this chapter is by no means a complete survey. Rather than trying to give a detailed account of methods in this area, I focus my discussion on the basic elements of these techniques that seem particularly useful for asset pricing. Subsequent chapters flesh out the material on some of those methods in more detail by looking at asset pricing applications.

2.1 SUPERVISED LEARNING AS FUNCTION APPROXIMATION

In supervised learning, the objective is to predict outcomes y (e.g., stock prices) based on some K observed predictors, or features, collected in the $K \times 1$ vector x (e.g., a set of firm characteristics). We can characterize this problem as using training data $\{y_i, x_i\}_1^N$ to find the unknown function $f \in \mathcal{F}$ in

$$y_i = f(x_i) + \varepsilon_i \qquad (2.1)$$

that maps predictors into outcomes, where ε represents mean-zero noise that is unpredictable by x. The hope is that outcomes encountered outside of the training data set will be generated from the same statistical model (2.1) as the training data so that the function estimate $\hat{f}(x_i)$ obtained from the training data will be a good out-of-sample predictor.

Supervised learning methods can be grouped into two categories. *Classification* methods are used in settings where the dependent variable y is categorial. *Regression* methods deal with continuous dependent variables. In asset pricing applications, regression problems are more common, although classification methods can also be useful, for example for prediction of binary events like a corporate default. I focus on regression methods in this book.

Supervised learning methods also differ in the class of functions $\mathcal{F}$ they consider. Some methods work with linear functions. Methods in this category are variants of linear regression methods that are ubiquitous in econometrics. Other methods allow for highly nonlinear functions. These methods have analogies with nonparameteric methods in econometrics such as kernel regression approaches. Common to all of these supervised learning methods is that they are designed to work well in high-dimensional settings where x includes a very large number of features, possibly greater than the number of observations in the training data.

ML researchers typically try to avoid making strong assumptions about f such as, for example, assuming that f is linear and x low-dimensional, with only a few variables selected a priori out of a much larger set of potential predictors. Instead, the goal is to let the data speak about $f(x_i)$ under only weak assumptions about f and about the set of relevant predictors. How far can one push this idea? Is it possible to develop a completely automated universal ML approach that can uncover f entirely from the data in any arbitrary setting (e.g., no matter whether the prediction problem is, say, in image recognition, biomedical applications, or asset pricing) and then provide predictions that generalize from the training data to test data sets that were not seen by the learning algorithm?

Wolpert (1996) shows that such a universal learning algorithm does not exist. This result is known as the *no-free-lunch* theorem in ML. This means that unless we have some prior knowledge about the prediction problem, we don't have reason to prefer, just based on first principles, one learning algorithm over another one. Moreover, if we have multiple algorithms that fit the training data equally well, we cannot determine, without prior knowledge, which of these is likely to yield better predictions on a yet-unseen test data set. Finding an algorithm that produces good predictions on the test data therefore necessarily requires some domain-specific prior knowledge about the prediction problem that we are trying to solve. In our supervised learning framework here, this could be knowledge about the class of functions that f belongs to, the stability of this function as we move from a training data set to a test data on which we want to make predictions, and the statistical distribution of ε and x. Successful prediction requires that we bias our choice of learning algorithm, including the details of its implementation, towards algorithms that are appropriate for the nature of the prediction problem we face (Wilson and Martinez 1997).

This connects to an underlying theme of this book. To successfully apply ML in asset pricing, we need to look for ways to bring in knowledge about the properties of asset price data when we choose among the many available learning algorithms and their various specifications. The number of learning algorithms and specification choices that we could take off the shelf to throw at a prediction problem is huge. But not all of these are equally well suited for prediction problems in asset pricing.

We now briefly review several supervised learning methods. Then, at the end of this chapter, and also in the next chapter, we return to the question of how to impose prior knowledge on the learning algorithm.

2.2   REGRESSION METHODS

Regression methods have a long tradition in statistics and econometrics. The novelty in many ML applications of these techniques is in the tweaks that have been applied to these methods to make them work well—in the sense of being computationally feasible and producing good predictive performance—in high-dimensional environments and in possibly highly nonlinear problems.

We start by reviewing linear models. For reasons that we discuss in more detail in Chapter 3, linear models probably have a more important role to play in asset pricing than in typical ML applications outside of finance. Moreover, linear models can be more flexible than it might seem. Methods that are formally linear can easily accommodate many types of nonlinearities through nonlinear transformations of predictor variables.

2.2.1   Linear Methods: Ridge Regression and Lasso

In a linear regression model, we assume that the function $f(x_i)$ is linear, i.e.,

$$y_i = x_i'g + \varepsilon_i, \tag{2.2}$$

where g is a vector of unknown regression coefficients. While the model is linear in terms of how y_i relates to the elements of x_i, the vector x_i could include nonlinear transformations of predictors.

One type of nonlinear transformation that we will come back to repeatedly in this book involves variable interactions. For example, if we start with an original 2×1 vector of features $h_i = (h_{1,i}, h_{2,i})'$, we could generate a vector $x_i = (h_{1,i}, h_{2,i}, h_{1,i}h_{2,i})'$ that includes the product $h_{1,i}h_{2,i}$ among the explanatory variables in the regression in order to capture interaction effects between the two original features.

Now suppose we have N observations in a training data set that we stack into an $N \times 1$ vector $y = (y_1, y_2, ..., y_N)'$ and $N \times K$ matrix $X = (x_1, x_2, ..., x_N)'$. A common way to estimate g is to choose a g that minimizes the sum of squared errors, i.e., our objective is

$$\min_g (y - Xg)'(y - Xg). \tag{2.3}$$

Differentiating with respect to g, setting the first derivative to zero, and solving for g, we obtain the ordinary least squares (OLS) estimator

$$\hat{g} = (X'X)^{-1}X'y, \tag{2.4}$$

and the in-sample fitted values

$$\hat{y} = X\hat{g}. \tag{2.5}$$

In high-dimensional settings, where K is not small relative to N, or perhaps even bigger than N, predictions based on OLS estimates often turn out to be unreliable. While the in-sample R^2 in this case can be very high, the R^2 for out-of-sample predictions can be very low or even negative. The reason is that with so many covariates relative to the number of observations, OLS greatly overfits the data by tweaking $\hat{g}$ to fit noise rather than true signal. These in-sample seemingly predictable patterns then do not repeat in an out-of-sample data set and the predictions perform poorly. In the extreme case with $K > N$, OLS estimates are not unique. There is an infinite number of solutions for $\hat{g}$ that all fit the training data perfectly. But much of this perfect fit may be spuriously fitting the ε_i in $y_i = f(x_i) + \varepsilon_i$ rather than capturing $f(x_i)$.

Ridge regression. When K is large, it can help predictive performance to penalize the estimator for picking large magnitudes of the elements of $\hat{g}$. Ridge regression is one example of such an approach. In Ridge regression (Hoerl and Kennard 1970), the objective is to minimize the same sum-of-squared-error loss function as in OLS, but augmented with a squared L^2-norm penalty $g'g$,

$$\min_g \left[\frac{1}{N}(y - Xg)'(y - Xg) + \gamma g'g \right]. \qquad (2.6)$$

Thus, the objective has two parts. The first term represents the *loss*. OLS regression would just minimize this part. The second term represents the penalty where the hyperparameter γ controls the strength of penalization. The solution is

$$\hat{g} = (X'X + \gamma I_K)^{-1} X'y, \qquad (2.7)$$

where I_K is a $K \times K$ identity matrix. By adding a diagonal matrix (a "ridge") to $X'X$, the presence of γI_K in the inverse induces shrinkage of the regression coefficients toward zero. Intuitively, the presence of the penalty term with $g'g$ in (2.6) penalizes estimates that have big magnitudes of the elements of $\hat{g}$. As a result, ridge regression ends up with regression coefficient estimates that are closer to zero than OLS estimates (OLS is the special case $\gamma = 0$). The L^2-shrinkage in ridge regression is an example of *regularization* to prevent overfitting.

In the special case of X with orthonormal columns, i.e., $X'X = I_K$, one can see from (2.7) that ridge regression shrinks each element of the coefficient estimate vector from the OLS estimate $\hat{g}_{j,OLS}$ toward zero by the same factor: $\hat{g}_j = \hat{g}_{j,OLS}/(1 + \gamma)$.

Lasso. An alternative and popular approach is to penalize with an L^1-norm penalty $\|g\|_1 = \sum_{j=1}^K |g_j|$ instead. This is the lasso method (Tibshirani 1996). The lasso objective is

$$\min_{g} \left[\frac{1}{N}(y - Xg)'(y - Xg) + \gamma \sum_{j=1}^{K} |g_j| \right]. \qquad (2.8)$$

Unlike in the ridge case, the solution is not linear in y and there is no closed-form expression for this solution, but several procedures exist that can solve numerically for the lasso solution, including the least angle regression (LARS) algorithm (Hastie, Tibshirani, and Friedman 2009).

As in the ridge regression case, this penalty specification also induces shrinkage of coefficients toward zero. But shrinkage is of a different nature here. Unlike ridge regression, the lasso can yield *sparse* coefficient estimates, where only a small number of the elements of $\hat{g}$ are nonzero.

In the special case of X with orthonormal columns, the lasso shifts OLS estimates toward zero by a fixed amount γ, but if doing so would flip the sign for an element of $\hat{g}$, this element is set to zero instead (Hastie, Tibshirani, and Friedman 2009). This means we have $\hat{g}_j = \text{sgn}(\hat{g}_{j,OLS})(|\hat{g}_{j,OLS}| - \gamma)_+$.

Elastic net. The lasso runs into problems with correlated variables. Suppose, for example, that we have two strongly positively correlated covariates that are both associated with a corresponding element of g that takes exactly the same true value. Whether we include only one or the other covariate among the nonzero coefficients (with coefficient estimate doubled relative to the true coefficient) or both (with the two coefficient estimates approximately equal to the true coefficients) affects approximately neither the loss part nor the penalty part of the lasso objective in (2.8). As a consequence, the lasso is nearly indifferent between including one, the other, or both covariates among those that get nonzero coefficients. It may depend on some irrelevant properties of noise in the data which of these options lasso will pick. Slight tweaks to the data could lead the lasso to flip from selecting one instead of the other variable. To maximize predictive performance, it may however be best to include an average of both covariates in the model, so that we average out the noise of the two covariates. This is precisely what ridge regression would do.

For this reason, the elastic net (Zou and Hastie 2005) combines ridge and lasso penalties

$$\min_{g} \left[\frac{1}{N}(y - Xg)'(y - Xg) + \gamma_1 \sum_{j=1}^{K} |g_j| + \gamma_2 g'g \right]. \qquad (2.9)$$

Like the lasso, the elastic net will set some coefficients to exactly zero, but it relies on variable selection to a lesser degree than the lasso and instead also imposes some ridge-like shrinkage.

One important issue that we will come back to in the next chapters is that the ridge, lasso, and elastic net solutions are not invariant to the scaling of the covariates. For example, in the ridge case, suppose that X is such that $X'X$ is diagonal. How much estimates get shrunk to zero when we add the ridge γI_K to $X'X$ depends on the magnitude of the diagonal elements of $X'X$. For covariates with small variance and hence a small diagonal entry in $X'X$, the effect of adding γ to the diagonal element is much bigger than for covariates with large variance. For this reason, it is common to standardize inputs to unit standard deviation before computing the ridge estimates. But this may not always be the right approach. Sometimes prior knowledge about a learning problem can tell us that we actually should shrink the coefficients of some covariates more than those of others.

2.2.2   Trees and Random Forests

Regression trees approximate the nonlinear function $f(x_i)$ with a multi-dimensional step function (Breiman, Friedman, Olshen, and Stone 1984). The feature space is divided into regions, or *leaves*, that contain a neighborhood around each point x_i at which we want to approximate f. Within each leaf $h = 1, ..., H$, the function $f(x_i)$ is approximated as an equal-weighted average, $\bar{y}_h$, of the observations y_i in this leaf.

Finding a suitable general partition of the feature space can be difficult. For this reason, tree-based algorithms often use recursive binary partitions. The partitioning of the feature can then be represented as a decision tree; hence the name of the method. Panel (a) in Figure 2.1 presents an example.

How can we find a partition that approximates f well? Finding the globally optimal partition that minimizes the residual sum of squared errors can be computationally infeasible. Even if we restrict ourselves to recursive binary partitions, there may still be an enormous number of possible trees that we would have to evaluate to determine global optimality. Much of the success of tree-based methods has come from the development of algorithms that do a good job in finding partitions that work well in applications, even though they typically do not find the globally optimal partition.

One common approach is a *greedy* algorithm (see, e.g., Hastie, Tibshirani, and Friedman 2009). Instead of evaluating global optimality, the algorithm walks through the tree and determines the best split based on a local assessment of fit at each step. More precisely, we start with all the data and we check for each feature what the residual sum of squared errors would be if we partitioned the sample into two regions just based on this feature and with a threshold that maximizes fit. We then choose to split based on the feature where we get the best fit. Within each of the resulting two regions, we then repeat this process. We keep doing this

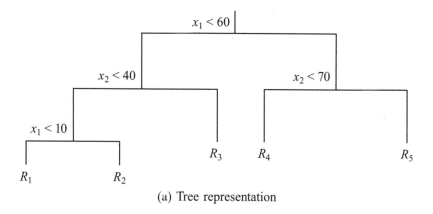

(a) Tree representation

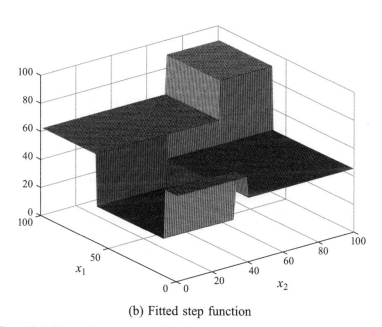

(b) Fitted step function

Figure 2.1. Regression tree example

until we have grown the tree to the point at which the number of observations within each region reaches a minimum number that we have set as a termination criterion at the start of the process.

Concretely, for the example tree in Figure 2.1, suppose in the first step that splitting on x_1 provides the biggest explanatory power compared with single splits based on the other features. We therefore split into two regions by applying a threshold to x_1. We choose the threshold such that it gives us the best fit, in terms of residual sum of squared errors, when we approximate f with the equal weighted average of y_i in the two regions left and right of the threshold. In the next step, suppose it turns out that splitting by x_2 in each branch delivers the best fit. We therefore split by x_2 into four regions, based on fit-maximizing thresholds that are specific to each branch of the tree. Finally, going through similar reasoning as in the previous steps, we split once more based on x_1 in the left branch of the tree, resulting in a total of $H = 5$ leaves. Let $R_1, R_2, ..., R_5$ denote the regions in terms of $x = (x_1, x_2)$ corresponding to the leaves. Panel (b) presents the fitted values, $\bar{y}_h$, calculated as the equal-weighed average of observations y_i within each leaf, i.e., for observations with $x_i \in R_h$.

The method is therefore conceptually similar to kernel regression. In a simple variant of kernel regression, predictions are also obtained by averaging observations in a neighborhood around the point of interest, but the definition of what constitutes a "neighborhood" and the weighting of data in this neighborhood are different in the tree method.

We could have carried the process further, resulting in a larger tree. So how far should we take the process of partitioning the feature space? A large tree has the advantage that it can more accurately approximate highly nonlinear functions. The downside is that it may overfit noise in the training data, resulting in poor out-of-sample prediction performance.

To balance accurate approximation of f with avoiding overfitting, we can start with a very large tree that would certainly overfit and then *prune* the tree by collapsing leaves. To develop a criterion for how much to prune the tree, we can add a penalty term to the residual sum of squares. Let H denote the number of leaves at the end of the tree. We can then look for a pruned tree that minimizes the penalized residual sum of squares

$$\sum_{h=1}^{H} \sum_{x_i \in R_h} (y_i - \bar{y}_h)^2 + \gamma H. \tag{2.10}$$

The tuning parameter γ controls how much we want to prune the tree. The value $\gamma = 0$ would imply no pruning, while higher values of γ imply more pruning.

A very popular alternative to penalization of tree size is to use *Random Forests* (Breiman 2001). In this case, we grow a tree to full size (up to some small minimum leaf size) without pruning and then apply bootstrap aggregation, or *bagging*, to reduce the overfitting. This works as follows. Suppose we have J features in x_i. First we draw a bootstrap sample from the training data that is of the same size as the original training data set. In this bootstrap sample, we then randomly select $m < J$ features at random and grow a tree until the minimum leaf size is reached. We record this tree and then draw another bootstrap sample from the original data to repeat the process. The fitted value at a point x_i is the average of the fitted values at x_i that we get from each individual tree. The constant m is a tuning parameter. Picking a value for it is similar to choosing a penalty parameter in penalized approaches.

Intuitively, each of the bootstrap samples has, to some extent, different noise. So if the fully grown trees are overfitting noise, their predictions will be affected by noise in different ways in different bootstrap samples. Moreover, the random selection of a subset of features in each bootstrap sample magnifies these differences. Taking the mean prediction across trees from different bootstrap samples averages out much of these noise-induced effects. Athey, Tibshirani, and Wager (2019) offer an interpretation analogous to kernel regression. Kernel regressions make predictions at point x_i by forming a weighted average of observations in a neighborhood around x_i, giving more weight to closer observations. Athey et al. show that averaging across trees in random forests has a somewhat similar effect in that closer points are included more often than distant points in the construction of the prediction at x_i.

2.2.3 Neural Networks

Neural networks are essentially methods to estimate highly nonlinear regression functions. For example, suppose we have J covariates x_i, which serve as *inputs* to the network and one dependent variable y_i, which is the *output*. Inputs and output are connected through a hidden layer of H *nodes* that we can think of as underlying latent variables. With $y_i = f(x_i) + \varepsilon_i$, the network can be expressed as

$$f(x_i) = a_2 + w_2'g(a_1 + W_1 x_i), \qquad (2.11)$$

where $a_1 + W_1 x_i$ represents the vector of latent variables. The *activation function* g is nonlinear and operates element-wise on each latent variable. For example, a popular choice is the Rectified Linear Unit (ReLU) where $g(z) = \max(0, z)$, which is a piecewise linear function that outputs an element of z directly if the element is positive, and outputs zero otherwise. The output of the activation function is then weighted by w_2 and shifted by a_2 to produce the final output $f(x_i)$ in the output layer.

The nonlinearity of g is crucial for the network to approximate nonlinear functions. If g were linear, e.g., $g(z) = Az$ for some matrix A, the network would collapse into a linear regression model $y_i = a + g'x_i + \varepsilon_i$ with $g' = w_2'AW_1$ and $a = a_2 + w_2'Aa_1$.

The number of hidden nodes controls the flexibility of the function approximation. With a large number of hidden nodes, one can approximate highly nonlinear functions arbitrarily well (Cybenko 1989; Hornik, Stinchcombe, and White 1989). Networks used for image recognition or natural language processing contain tens or hundreds of thousands of nodes (LeCun, Bengio, and Hinton 2015).

One can add additional layers. For example, with two hidden layers we have

$$f(x_i) = a_3 + w_3 g(a_2 + W_2 g(a_1 + W_1 x_i)). \tag{2.12}$$

Deep neural networks add several such layers, often 10 to 20. The result is a network that has a sequence of linear mappings with interwoven nonlinear transformations. The number of parameters can be very large. For example, with a single hidden layer with H nodes, one output, and J inputs, the total number of parameters in W_1, a_1, and a_2 is $H \times J + H + 1$. With $J = 1000$ inputs and $H = 10000$ hidden nodes, this would amount to more than ten million parameters. For a fully connected network, each added layer with the same number of hidden nodes adds another $H \times H + H$ parameters.

In principle, networks with a single hidden layer can approximate any nonlinear function. In practice, though, with typical data sets, adding layers to a network often seems to lead to better performance. Whether deep networks with many layers are generally better is still an open question (see, e.g., Ba and Caruana (2013)). Lin, Tegmark, and Rolnick (2017) argue that certain properties of the data and functions to be approximated matter. For example, deep networks are well suited for approximating functions that have a hierarchical structure.

Interaction effects—i.e., situations where the joint effect of multiple inputs on the output is not additive—are a type of nonlinearity that may be particularly relevant for the asset pricing applications that we start discussing in the next chapter. It is therefore useful to take a closer look at how such interactions can be captured by a neural network.

Consider a network with a single hidden layer as in (2.11) with two nodes. Suppose further that $a_2 = 0$, $w_2 = (1, 1)'$, $a_1 = (-3/2, -3/2)'$, the first row of W_1 is $(1, 1)$ and the second row is $(-1, -1)$, and $g(z) = \max(0, z)$, i.e.,

$$f(x_i) = \max(0, -3/2 + x_{i,1} + x_{i,2}) + \max(0, -3/2 - x_{i,1} - x_{i,2}). \tag{2.13}$$

In this case, the first term only "activates" if the sum of the two features $x_{i,1}$ and $x_{i,2}$ is large enough; otherwise it is zero. The second term only "activates" if the sum of the two features $x_{i,1}$ and $x_{i,2}$ is small enough. The result is the function shown in Figure 2.2.

By adding additional hidden nodes, we could add additional piecewise linear parts to this function, for example for larger values of $x_{i,1} + x_{i,2}$ and more strongly negative values of $-x_{i,1} - x_{i,2}$. In this way, the neural

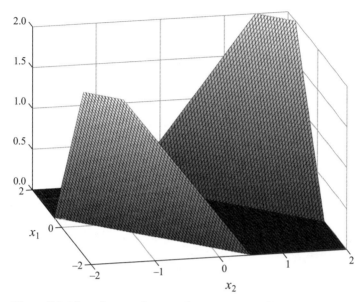

Figure 2.2. Neural network example: Interaction effects

network could approximate, for example, a function like $(x_{i,1} + x_{i,2})^2 = x_{i,1}^2 + 2x_{i,1}x_{i,2} + x_{i,2}^2$ that involves cross-feature interactions $x_{i,1}x_{i,2}$.

To fit neural network using training data, one can use a sum-of-squared errors objective similar to the one we discussed earlier for linear regression methods. Collecting all parameters of the network in the vector θ, the objective is

$$\min_{\theta} \sum_{i=1}^{N} [y_i - f(x_i, \theta)]^2. \tag{2.14}$$

Minimization of this objective can be carried out with numerical methods such as stochastic gradient descent or quasi-Newton methods (see Hastie, Tibshirani, and Friedman 2009). For the purpose of minimization, it can also be advantageous to use a smooth activation function such as the sigmoid function instead of a non-differentiable function such as ReLU.[1]

For neural networks, too, we need to worry about overfitting the training data. A network with many nodes and layers might approximate the training data extremely well but perform poorly in predicting out-of-sample. Regularization can prevent such overfitting. Analogously to adding the penalty term in the ridge regression objective (2.6), we can

---

[1] The sigmoid function $g(z_i) = [1 + \exp(-z_i)]^{-1}$ takes values in the interval $(0, 1)$ and approaches asymptotes of 0 and 1 for $z_i \to -\infty$ and $z_i \to +\infty$, respectively.

add a squared L^2-norm penalty term to the objective here:

$$\min_{\theta} \sum_{i=1}^{N} [y_i - f(x_i, \theta)]^2 + \gamma \theta' \theta. \qquad (2.15)$$

This has the effect of shrinking the neural network weights toward zero. With a sigmoid activation function, very small weights imply that the activation function is in a region where it is approximately linear. So not only is the output shrunk toward zero, but the neural network is also shrunk toward a linear regression model.

As in the case of the linear regression methods we discussed earlier, scaling of inputs matters here for the effects of regularization. Greater absolute magnitude of an input would mean lower magnitudes of the weights associated with this input on the path on which it feeds through the network, and hence a smaller role of these weights in the penalty term $\gamma \theta' \theta$ and therefore less shrinkage applied to them. It is common to scale inputs to have mean zero and unit standard deviation, but this is not necessarily the best approach. Based on a priori considerations about the prediction problem and the properties of the data, it could be preferable to have different inputs scaled to different magnitudes in order to increase the degree of shrinkage for some elements of θ and reduce it for others.

2.3 Hyperparameter Tuning

The learning algorithms that we discussed so far involve hyperparameters that need to be preset before training. For example, the ridge regression objective (2.6) depends on the hyperparameter γ that determines the weight on the penalty term in the objective, and hence the degree of shrinkage induced by the penalty. To estimate the regression coefficients g from the training data, we need to fix a value of γ beforehand. Similarly, the lasso requires a preset penalty parameter, and the elastic net estimator requires two. As we just discussed in the previous section, neural network objective functions can have penalty parameters, too. For random forests, the size of the randomly drawn set of candidate features to split nodes on and the maximum depth of the trees are hyperparameters, for example.

Ultimately, we are interested in having the trained model perform well in prediction tasks. For this reason, we seek hyperparameter values that minimize the prediction error. In order to minimize prediction error, we need to be able to estimate the prediction error for a given value of the hyperparameter. This is not entirely straightforward. We cannot simply use the in-sample error in the training data set, because it is a downward biased estimate of the prediction error that we obtain in a new data set not used for training the model. In the ridge regression case, for example, with a ridge regression estimate of $\hat{g}(\gamma)$ and squared error loss, the in-sample error is

$$mse(\gamma) = \frac{1}{N}[y - X\hat{g}(\gamma)]'[y - X\hat{g}(\gamma)]. \tag{2.16}$$

Within the training data, the ridge regression estimate $\hat{g}$ fits not only the variation in y truly related to X, but also to some extent the noise in the residual ε. To what extent an estimated model can (over-)fit the noise in the training data depends on the model's complexity. One approach to estimating the expected out-of-sample prediction error therefore tries to correct the in-sample error for the bias induced by the model's complexity. In an OLS regression, the complexity would simply be the number of parameters that are estimated, which in turn is equal to the number of covariates. In the ridge regression case, the situation is a bit more complicated, because shrinkage constrains the estimates and thereby reduces model complexity. When we look for an optimal ridge regression penalty, we do not simply pick γ to minimize $mse(\gamma)$, but also take into account the out-of-sample prediction benefits of reduced model complexity that come with a higher γ.

For linear models where the fitted values can be expressed as $\hat{y} = Hy$, one can capture model complexity with the effective number of parameters equal to the trace of the "hat"-matrix H (Hastie, Tibshirani, and Friedman 2009). In the ridge regression case, this effective number of parameters is

$$d(\gamma) = \text{tr}\left[X(X'X + \gamma I_K)^{-1}X'\right] \tag{2.17}$$

where tr[.] represents the trace operator. In the OLS case, where $\gamma = 0$, d would simply be equal to the number of covariates included in the regression, i.e., $d = K$.[2] With $\gamma > 0$, we have $d < K$. Shrinkage reduces the effective number of parameters. For example, in the special case of X with orthonormal columns, we would have $d = K/(1 + \gamma)$.

Equipped with the effective number of parameters, we can then calculate measures of fit that adjust the in-sample error for its optimistic bias and that account for the complexity-reducing benefit of a higher penalty. The adjusted measures should be a better estimate of the expected prediction error than the in-sample error. One such measure is the Akaike information criterion (AIC). In the case of a ridge regression and under the assumption that ε represents uncorrelated Gaussian noise, the AIC is

$$AIC(\gamma) = N \log mse(\gamma) + 2d(\gamma). \tag{2.18}$$

---

[2]To see this, use the cyclical properties of the trace, which imply $\text{tr}[X(X'X)^{-1}X'] = \text{tr}[X'X(X'X)^{-1}] = \text{tr}(I_K) = K$.

The first term increases as we increase γ, while the second term shrinks. We can take the γ that minimizes the sum of the two terms as our hyperparameter estimate $\hat{\gamma}$.

While the AIC can sometimes be helpful to get an approximate idea of the expected prediction error, and hyperparameter values that minimize it, it has some shortcomings as well. For nonlinear models, getting a measure of model complexity, or the effective number of parameters, is more difficult than for a linear model. And even for linear models, the AIC relies on strong assumptions. The expression for the AIC in (2.18) requires that the elements of $\boldsymbol{\varepsilon}$ be independently and identically normally distributed. In case of deviations from this assumption, we would need to specify the exact form of the likelihood in order to implement the AIC.

For these reasons, ML practitioners often prefer alternative approaches to prediction error estimation and hyperparameter tuning that are less demanding in terms of underlying assumptions. A popular purely data-driven method is cross-validation (CV). In CV, the model estimates obtained from the training data are used to make predictions on a separate, independent validation data set. The model's error on this validation data set then provides an estimate of the prediction error. CV seems like a natural method for assessing predictive performance: we simply check the actual predictive performance on a data set that we didn't use to train the model. Moreover, Stone (1977) showed that model comparisons based on CV or AIC are asymptotically equivalent. In this sense, we can think of CV as empirically approximating the AIC.

Using the CV approach, we can use the prediction error in the validation data as the objective to minimize when we tune hyperparameters. For example, in the case of ridge regression, we use the estimates $\hat{g}(\gamma)$ that we obtained from the training data for a given value of γ to construct fitted values and prediction errors on a validation data set (X_v, y_v) that is independent from the training data set, i.e., we calculate $y_v - X_v \hat{g}(\gamma)$. We then look for a value of γ that minimizes the sum of squared prediction errors in the validation data, i.e.,

$$\hat{\gamma} = \arg_\gamma \min [y_v - X_v \hat{g}(\gamma)]'[y_v - X_v \hat{g}(\gamma)]. \qquad (2.19)$$

In many cases, just performing a simple split of the available data into one training and one validation sample is not an efficient use of the data. The method of k-fold CV seeks to improve the efficiency of prediction error estimation by using the entire data set for training and validation. The method achieves this by splitting the data set into k parts, or "folds," that are usually equally sized. We then use one of the k folds for model validation and the remaining $k - 1$ folds for model estimation. Then we pick another one of the k folds for validation and the remaining folds for estimation, and so on, until we have used all the k folds exactly once for validation. We use the average of the prediction errors from the k validation folds as our estimate of the expected prediction error. We then search for hyperparameter values that minimize this estimated expected prediction error. In the example of ridge regression, we would look for a value of γ such that

$$\hat{\gamma} = \arg_\gamma \min \frac{1}{k} \sum_{j=1}^{k} [y_{v(j)} - X_{v(j)}\hat{g}_{-v(j)}(\gamma)]'[y_{v(j)} - X_{v(j)}\hat{g}_{-v(j)}(\gamma)]. \quad (2.20)$$

Here $v(j) = 1, 2, ..., k$ denotes an index of the k folds that the data set has been divided into, while $-v(j)$ refers to the remaining part of the data set that is not in the j-th fold.

How many folds should we use? There is no clear guidance on this question in the ML literature. Broadly speaking, there is a trade-off. Keeping k very small means that we use smaller training data sets to estimate the model. This handicaps the model by reducing the amount of data used to estimate its parameters. The consequence is a pessimistically biased assessment of the prediction error. On the other hand, large k means that the training data set used in each of the k estimation runs is overlapping to a large degree. In this case, there is the concern that the full data set that the estimation and validation folds are taken from is somewhat special in its properties and therefore the prediction error we estimate from large k-CV is special as well. If we looked at an independent draw of a new data set, and used this one to train the model, perhaps we would typically get a higher or lower prediction error than on our original data set. CV with small k protects us from this possibility to some extent because it effectively uses quite different draws of training data sets that are not so strongly overlapping. In this sense, there is a bias-variance trade-off (Hastie, Tibshirani, and Friedman 2009): large k means that we get a close to unbiased estimate of the prediction error, but one with high variance—which here means a high degree of uncertainty about how the prediction error would look on a newly drawn data set used for training.

While this trade-off is clear conceptually, there is no clear guidance on where the optimum is in a particular application. It likely depends on the properties of the data and the algorithm being trained. In addition, CV with large k is computationally intensive. It requires k repetitions of model training and validation, which can be prohibitive on large data sets. In practice it is therefore common to choose values of k that are far smaller than the number of observations.

In interpreting the prediction error that we obtain in the k validation folds, we need to keep in mind that we used these folds to estimate γ. Since we pick $\hat{\gamma}$ to minimize the prediction errors in the validation folds, the average prediction error from the validation folds for this estimate of γ should be an optimistically biased estimate of the expected prediction error. For this reason, we might want to reserve another part of the data as a test data set that was used neither for model training nor for hyperparameter tuning and evaluate the prediction error on this test data set.

2.4 BAYESIAN INTERPRETATION

Application of ML methods requires a number of choices. Even if we fix the model that we want to train—e.g., a linear regression or a neural network—we face a number of possibilities on how to regularize the estimation. For example, in penalized regression, the choice of penalty function will determine whether the estimated model will likely feature sparsity (if we use an L^1-norm penalty) or not (if we use a squared L^2-norm penalty). Which one is best? Having made this choice, we then need to tune the penalty hyperparameters, as we just discussed in the previous section. Choices concerning variable scaling are important, too. In this chapter we have already encountered the issue that the effect of penalization on parameter estimates is sensitive to the scaling of the input variables. Should we normalize all inputs to have equal standard deviation or would some other type of scaling be better? The answer is not obvious.

We could try to simply let the data speak on these questions. Just as we can optimize hyperparameters with CV, we could try to use CV to find out which of these choices works best in terms of producing lower prediction error on a validation data set. Ultimately, though, we would run into the no-free lunch problem (Wolpert 1996) emphasized at the beginning of this chapter: we cannot hope to identify one ML algorithm that is universally better than any other algorithm over all possible data generating distributions. We will have to make some a priori assumptions about the properties of the data. A purely data-driven ML approach is not possible. We need to bring in some prior knowledge about the objective we are pursuing with the ML approach and the kinds of data that the algorithm will be confronted with.

A Bayesian interpretation of parameter estimation and regularization can be helpful for this purpose. Bayesian statistics allows us to express prior knowledge probabilistically, in terms of prior distributions. Consider the linear regression framework $y = Xg + \varepsilon$ and assume that $\varepsilon \sim \mathcal{N}(0, \Sigma)$, where we know the values of entries in the covariance matrix Σ, but not the value of the coefficient vector g. Prior knowledge comes in the form of a prior distribution for g. Under certain assumptions, we can map Bayesian estimation into the ridge and lasso regressions we discussed earlier in this chapter. As we show now, the specification of the prior distribution affects the type of penalization that is imposed on the objective function.

Suppose we have the view that the elements of g are drawn from a multivariate normal distribution, $g \sim \mathcal{N}(0, \Sigma_g)$. Given this prior distribution, $p(g)$, and the likelihood, $p(y|g)$, implied by the normal distribution of the regression residuals ε, Bayes' rule tells us that the posterior distribution of g given the observed data y follows

$$p(g|y) \propto p(y|g)p(g). \tag{2.21}$$

With normal prior and likelihood, the posterior distribution is normal, too. The mean of this posterior distribution takes a form akin to a generalized least-squares (GLS) regression, but with an additional term in the inverse (Lindley and Smith 1972):

$$\hat{g} = \left(X'\Sigma^{-1}X + \Sigma_g^{-1}\right)^{-1} X'\Sigma^{-1}y. \tag{2.22}$$

The additional term Σ_g^{-1} in the inverse induces shrinkage that tilts the estimates away from the GLS estimates toward the mean of the prior distribution (which we assumed to be a vector of zeros here). If we specialize to uncorrelated homoskedastic regression residuals, $\Sigma = I_N \sigma^2$, and uncorrelated and homoskedastic elements of g under the prior distribution, $\Sigma_g = I_K \sigma_g^2$, we obtain

$$\hat{g} = \left(X'X + \frac{\sigma^2}{\sigma_g^2} I_K\right)^{-1} X'y. \tag{2.23}$$

This expression is identical to the ridge regression estimator in (2.7) with $\gamma = \sigma^2/\sigma_g^2$. This means that the ridge regression penalty has a Bayesian interpretation that relates γ to the dispersion in the prior distribution. If σ_g^2 is large, which implies that we do not have a precise prior view about the likely magnitude of the elements of g, γ is small and there is little shrinkage toward the prior mean. In contrast, if the prior distribution is tightly concentrated around the prior mean, with σ_g^2 small, then shrinkage is strong.

The Bayesian framework allows us to give a more precise interpretation of the concern about "overfitting" that we used earlier to motivate regularization and shrinkage. Overfitting means estimating a model without giving proper weight to prior information that we have about the parameters. If our prior is diffuse, $\sigma_g^2 \to \infty$, there is really no motivation for shrinkage. In this case, fitting a regression without shrinkage is not overfitting the training data. Speaking of overfitting only makes sense if there is reason to think—perhaps based on economic plausibility considerations—that the magnitude of the regression coefficients is unlikely to be extremely large. Then, ignoring such information and estimating a regression without shrinkage would mean that we are overfitting the training data by not giving any weight to this prior information.

Throughout much of this book, we will come back repeatedly to this Bayesian interpretation of regularization. In the ML literature, it is more common to discuss the effects of regularization in terms of a *bias-variance tradeoff*. Under this perspective, fitting an estimator to training data without much regularization yields low bias, but high estimation error, i.e., high variance. Regularization can reduce variance, but at the cost of biasing the estimator. From a Bayesian perspective, however, the frequentist notion of unbiased estimation that serves as a reference point for these tradeoff calculations is not of any particular significance. Given prior beliefs, the posterior, and the regularization implied by the posterior, represent the optimal way to combine these prior beliefs and the information from the empirical data. For the purpose of looking for links between regularization and economic restrictions—a central theme in this book—it is more useful to discuss how prior information shapes regularization than to frame it in terms of a bias-variance tradeoff.

The Bayesian interpretation of regularization also clarifies how we should think about scaling of covariates in a ridge regression. If one wants to use ridge regression, variables should be scaled in such a way that a prior that assigns equal variance to each element of g is plausible. In contrast, if we believe that some coefficients are likely smaller in magnitude than others, then ridge regression does not yield the appropriate degree of shrinkage. It shrinks too much the coefficients on covariates with coefficients likely far from zero relative to those that are likely closer to zero. We should then rescale the covariates such that equal variance of the elements of g becomes plausible. This is the point where we need to bring in domain-specific prior knowledge about the prediction task and the data-generating distribution in order to guide the estimator.

In the Bayesian framework, our prior view about the distribution of g also determines whether we end up with ridge regression or some other type of shrinkage. If the prior distribution is Laplace instead of normal, we obtain something close to the lasso. Figure 2.3 provides an example to compare the normal distribution (dashed line) with the Laplace distribution (solid line). Compared to the normal distribution, the Laplace distribution has more mass concentrated around zero and fatter tails. As a consequence, a Bayesian regression with Laplace prior leads, relative to ridge regression, to less shrinkage of large coefficients and greater shrinkage of small coefficients, which is similar to what the lasso does.

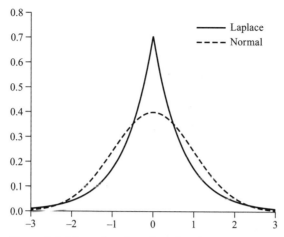

Figure 2.3. Normal and Laplace distributions

The posterior mean in Bayesian regression with Laplace prior does not exhibit sparsity, though. The lasso estimator—which yields sparse estimates—is not equal to the posterior mean but the posterior mode. This means that one obtains the lasso as a maximum a posteriori (MAP) estimator of g (Tibshirani 1996). The lasso penalty parameter effectively controls the dispersion of the prior distribution.

From Bayes' rule we can see that the MAP estimator is closely related to maximum likelihood estimation. The MAP estimator looks for the value of g that is most likely given the observed data and the prior beliefs, which means the value that maximizes the posterior probability

$$\hat{g} = \arg\max_{g} p(g|y), \tag{2.24}$$

which, by Bayes' rule is equivalent to maximizing $p(y|g)p(g)$, i.e., the product of the likelihood and the prior. In contrast, the maximum likelihood estimator would just maximize $p(y|g)$, without weighting by the prior distribution. In the case of a flat prior, the MAP and maximum likelihood estimator coincide.

While prediction based on MAP estimates is not a proper full-fledged Bayesian analysis—the fully Bayesian approach would use the posterior distribution to construct a predictive distribution, not point estimates plugged into the model, and it would incorporate prior uncertainty about σ^2—the MAP estimation framework allows us incorporate prior beliefs in a simple way. This in turn allows us to see how the lasso implicitly incorporates prior beliefs about g.

The same issue we discussed regarding the scaling of covariates for ridge regression applies to the lasso as well. When we apply the lasso, we implicitly express the view that a Laplace distribution with equal dispersion for each of the elements of g is the appropriate prior distribution. If we do not think this is a plausible assumption, we need to rescale the covariates accordingly. The off-the-shelf approach of standardizing covariates before lasso estimation is not necessarily the right approach.

Finally, we can give cross-validation a heuristic Bayesian interpretation as well. CV is essentially a way of estimating the prior dispersion σ_g^2 from the data. As we already discussed earlier, there is a connection between the complexity penalty imposed by the AIC and penalty choice based on CV. George and Foster (2000) show that there is in turn a close relationship between estimation that optimizes the AIC (or related measures of fit that impose a complexity penalty) and empirical Bayes estimation. In the empirical Bayes approach, the prior parameters are estimated empirically by putting an uninformative hyperprior on the prior parameters and then looking for prior parameter values that maximize the posterior probability. We can think of CV therefore as approximating an empirical Bayes approach in which we estimate parameters of the prior distribution from the data.

In summary, regularization has a Bayesian interpretation as the expression of prior knowledge about model parameters. Even if we do not formally follow a full Bayesian approach, we can use the Bayesian interpretation to bring domain-specific knowledge to bear on the learning problem. Preprocessing of data (e.g., scaling), or the specification of penalties (e.g., which kind of norm of the parameter vector to penalize), implicitly expresses prior views. The Bayesian interpretation can help us make these choices in a way that is appropriate for the specific ML problem we intend to tackle. In the next chapter, we examine properties of typical prediction problems in asset pricing and what these properties tell us, through a Bayesian lens, about appropriate preprocessing and specification choices.

Chapter 3

SUPERVISED LEARNING IN ASSET PRICING

THE SUPERVISED ML methods we reviewed in Chapter 2 are potentially valuable additions to the toolkit in asset pricing. Many prediction problems in asset pricing are of high-dimensional nature in that a large number of observable variables could have useful predictive information. For example, in stock return prediction a huge number of variables could potentially be relevant as predictors. Firm characteristics from accounting data, signals extracted from textual information in corporate disclosures, variables summarizing the history of price and trading volume, information in media reports, and many other variables could potentially contain predictive information.

Until recently, much of the existing literature in asset pricing has dealt with this high dimensionality by imposing ad hoc sparsity. Rather than considering large numbers of predictors simultaneously, researchers often consider small sets of predictors in isolation. For example, when researchers investigate a new predictor variable, a common approach in the academic literature is to evaluate whether the variable has marginal predictive information relative to a small "standard" set of firm characteristics, for instance, those used in the factors models of Hou, Xue, and Zhang (2015) and Fama and French (2015) (size, book-to-market equity, investment, profitability). The problem with this approach of considering small sets of predictors in isolation is that there could be substantial redundancy among the predictors that have been discovered in the literature.

There is no compelling economic motivation for the ad hoc sparsity imposed in this traditional approach. Accordingly, there is a need for approaches that can handle the high dimensionality of the prediction problem without imposing ad hoc sparsity. ML methods are well suited for this task, but straight off-the-shelf application of these methods is unlikely to fully exploit their potential. Asset pricing applications are in important ways different from the applications, often in the technology sector, for which the ML methods have originally been developed. Table 3.1 lists some of these differences. Of course, these distinctions are not always so clear-cut, but in many cases they will be relevant to some degree.

TABLE 3.1

Differences between typical ML and asset pricing applications

	Typical ML Application	Asset Pricing
Signal-to-noise	High	Very low
Data dimensions	Many predictors, Many observations	Many predictors Few observations
Aggregation level of interest	Individual outcomes	Portfolio outcomes
Prediction error covariances	Statistical nuisance	Important determinant of portfolio risk
Sparsity	Often sparse	Unclear
Structural change	None	Investors learn from data and adapt

Perhaps the most important difference is in the signal-to-noise ratio in typical data sets. In many typical ML applications, the algorithm can be trained with data in which the true outcomes are known. For example, in an image classification task like the one we discussed in Chapter 1, a training data set would consist of images whose true classification is known. Sticking to the example we discussed in Chapter 1, if the task is to classify images into the classes {hot dog, not hot dog}, we would train the algorithm with images that are correctly labeled as "hot dog" or "not hot dog." In contrast, in a return prediction application, a training data set would only be able to feed the algorithm the realized returns, r_{t+1}, of some assets, not their expected return, $\mathbb{E}_t[r_{t+1}]$. The expected return is unobservable. All we can see is the realized return as a noisy signal about the expected return. And in typical asset return data sets, variation in $\mathbb{E}_t[r_{t+1}]$ across assets or across time accounts only for a small share of the total variance of realized returns. As a consequence, the signal-to-noise ratio is very low.

The low signal-to-noise ratio problem is further compounded by the limitations of the data available to train models. Historical databases of asset returns only cover several decades. It may be tempting to think that high-frequency data can help to increase the number of observations by chopping return measurement periods into finer intervals. But this typically does not help for estimating $\mathbb{E}_t[r_{t+1}]$. Unless the predictable component of assets' returns is changing at high frequency—which seems implausible, unless we are trying to capture some market microstructure-induced predictability—we do not gain much, in terms of statistical power, by increasing the measurement frequency. This is related to the observation in Merton (1980) that increasing the measurement frequency does not yield more precise estimates of expected returns. Thus, one way or another, we have to live with the limited returns data availability.

In asset pricing, unlike in many typical ML applications, we are not necessarily interested in obtaining accurate predictions of individual outcomes. For example, in stock return prediction, we are not necessarily interested in predicting individual stocks' returns, but rather in constructing a portfolio with good risk-return properties. Whether methods that deliver the most accurate return forecasts at the individual stock level also automatically give us the best-performing portfolio once we aggregate across stocks is an open question that does not have an obvious answer, as we will see later in this chapter.

Because of this portfolio perspective in many asset pricing applications, we are also inherently more interested in the covariance properties of prediction errors than the data scientists working on typical ML problems. After all, in a setting with many assets, covariances of return prediction errors determine much of the portfolio volatility. And this portfolio volatility plays a big role in determining the risk-return properties of the portfolio. Properties of error covariances could matter at all stages of an ML application in asset pricing, starting with the question of what the optimal ML algorithm is, how to regularize it, how to evaluate predictive performance, and how to use its output for portfolio construction.

As we discussed in the previous chapter, for ML algorithms to work well, it is important to bring in prior knowledge about the nature of the prediction problem and the properties of the data. For regression problems, one such property is the degree of sparsity of the model. As Hastie, Tibshirani, and Wainwright (2015) emphasize, sparse models seem to do well in many applications, including genomics, image classification, textual analysis, and many others. In many of these applications, there are prior reasons to expect sparsity. For instance, in image classification, some regions of an image may simply be irrelevant for the classification task. Similarly, in analysis of genetic factors that predict a disease, a large number of candidate genes may have no relationship to the disease whatsoever. In asset pricing, however, it is not so clear, a priori, that a sparse model describes well how the data are generated. For example, in return prediction with accounting variables, what would be the justification for us to assume, before looking at the data, that a substantial number of balance sheet variables are likely to be completely irrelevant for return prediction? Wouldn't it be more plausible that some are more relevant, others less—perhaps because they are all different noisy signals of some underlying unobservable factors—but few are probably, a priori, of exactly zero relevance?

Finally, a fundamental difference between asset pricing and standard ML applications is that the asset prices that we feed into a learning algorithm are the outcome of investment decisions (by humans or machines) that are themselves informed by past data. As a consequence, the underlying processes generating the returns are unlikely to be stationary. For example, suppose a particular variable x is a good forecaster of returns in time periods leading up to some time t. At time t, investors discover this predictability and trade on it aggressively, with the consequence that the return predictability disappears in subsequent periods. Consider an analyst at time $T > t$ who studies the predictability of returns with a data set that extends until T, but also includes time periods prior to t. The analyst operates under the assumption that there is a stable underlying return-generating process that an ML algorithm can approximate. The trained algorithm in this case is unlikely to yield useful return forecasts at time T or later. The training data includes observations that have been rendered obsolete by the fact that investors have discovered the predictability associated with this variable x. In many typical ML applications, this type of problem does not exist because the data are generated in a stationary environment. There are no endogenous mechanisms whereby availability of data and its use in decision making leads to a subsequent change in the properties of the data. For example, returning to our image classification example with hot dogs, the hot dogs are not going to change shape or color in response to the analysis of hot dog image data. Perhaps for this reason, there is not much guidance yet from the ML literature on how one could adapt ML algorithms to deal with the structural changes over time that are likely to show up in asset price data.

In this chapter, we use a simple return prediction problem to illustrate in more detail some of the specific issues that arise when we apply ML methods in asset pricing. Fundamental questions, such as how to measure predictive performance, how to preprocess data, how to regularize estimators, and how to deal with structural change, are still largely unanswered. The goal of this chapter is to outline the challenges that need to be addressed.

3.1 EXAMPLE: CROSS-SECTIONAL STOCK RETURN PREDICTION

Return prediction plays a central role in the asset pricing literature. Academic researchers use return prediction regressions to study the determinants of risk premia and the degree of market efficiency. In quantitative investment management applications, return prediction models provide an important input for the design of investment strategies.

In this chapter, we look at a simple return prediction model for stocks that uses only past returns as predictors. A model with such a limited set of inputs is not meant to be representative of the sort of model that one would need to estimate in order to build a well-performing investment strategy in today's markets. A well-performing strategy based on such easily available inputs would be low-hanging fruit—but this fruit has likely been picked already quite a while ago. For our purposes here, an exploration of a simple returns-based prediction model with historical data is useful for illustrating some of the issues we have to tackle if we want to adopt ML techniques in asset pricing.

At a general level, the goal of return prediction regressions is to approximate conditional expected returns, which means that we are trying to find the function $f(.)$

$$\mathbb{E}[r_{i,t+1}|x_{i,t}] = f(x_{i,t}) \tag{3.1}$$

that maps observable asset-level characteristics $x_{i,t}$ into expectations of returns conditional on characteristics. We focus here purely on predicting *cross-sectional* differences in returns and so we can think of the returns of an individual stock, r_i, as expressed relative to a market index return. In the next chapter, we will look at a broader set of predictor variables, but here we start with a set of predictors composed exclusively of functions of past realized returns of stock i. Even within this restricted set of predictors, it is easy to come up with a large number of predictor variables, and hence a fairly high-dimensional prediction problem, if one doesn't want to impose ad hoc sparsity restrictions on the model.

Specifically, we analyze a model where $r_{i,t+1}$ is a monthly stock return and $f(x_{i,t})$ is a linear function of 120 lags of the stock's own past monthly returns, past returns squared, and past returns to the third power. The second and third power terms allow for possible nonlinearity in the relationship between past returns and future returns. To avoid contamination with microstructure-induced biases and very short horizons, we skip the first lag. Thus, we have the regression

$$r_{i,t+1} = \sum_{k=1}^{119} b_k r_{i,t-k} + \sum_{k=1}^{119} c_k r_{i,t-k}^2 + \sum_{k=1}^{119} d_k r_{i,t-k}^3 + e_{i,t+1}, \tag{3.2}$$

with a total of $3 \times 119 = 357$ predictor variables.

Each month t, we use all stocks in the Center for Research in Security Prices (CRSP) database except small stocks that have market capitalization below the 20th NYSE percentile and price lower than one dollar at the end of month $t - 1$. We exclude stocks below this threshold to make sure the results are not driven by extremely small and illiquid stocks. For the dependent variable $r_{i,t+1}$, we use returns from January 1970 to June

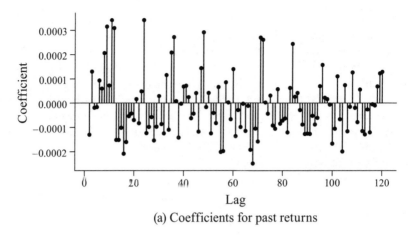

(a) Coefficients for past returns

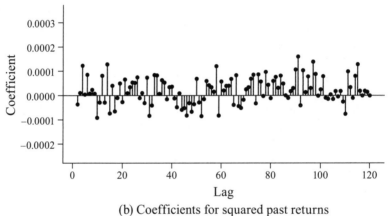

(b) Coefficients for squared past returns

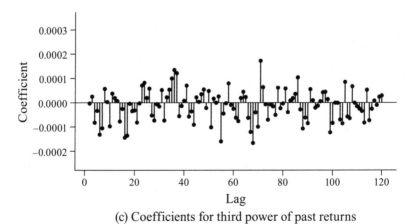

(c) Coefficients for third power of past returns

Figure 3.1. Ridge regression coefficient estimates

2019. We demean the dependent variable and all explanatory variables month by month to focus purely on cross-sectional variation (which is why the regression (3.2) does not include an intercept term). In addition, we cross-sectionally standardize all predictor variables to unit standard deviation each month. We weight the observations each month such that the regression gives equal weight to each month in the sample. In an asset pricing application with an unbalanced panel of stock returns, this is a natural weighting scheme because the mean return of a portfolio strategy (which might include a different number of stocks each month) would also give equal weight to each period.

We use the ridge regression estimator (2.7) that we discussed in the previous chapter. The penalty hyperparameter is estimated using leave-one-year-out CV. That is, the CV folds are contiguous blocks of monthly cross-sections that comprise a calendar year. This means that we compute the estimates using all but one year of the sample as training folds, we calculate the predicted returns in the left-out validation year, and we record the resulting R^2. We then repeat with a different left-out year and again record the R^2. We repeat until each year of the sample has been left out once. At the end, we average the R^2 across all left-out years and we search for a penalty value that maximizes this cross-validated R^2. This leave-one-year-out approach of constructing the folds is consistent with our data-weighting scheme that gives equal weight to each calendar period in the estimation.

To demonstrate that the ridge regression estimates recover useful information, we first inspect the estimated regression coefficients. The ridge regression automatically detects many prominent predictability patterns that have been documented in the existing literature for roughly this sample period or parts of it. Panel (a) of Figure 3.1 shows the estimates for the b_k coefficients in (3.2), i.e., the coefficients for the first-order terms of lagged returns. It may not be apparent at first sight, but on closer look one can see that in just one estimation, the ridge regression recovers several major anomalies related to past returns: the positive coefficients up to lags of 12 months capture momentum as in Jegadeesh and Titman (1993); the plot also shows that continuation of recent returns is concentrated in lags 6 to 12, as pointed out in Novy-Marx (2012); the mostly negative coefficients for lags beyond 12 months reflect long-term reversals as in DeBondt and Thaler (1985). Strikingly, there are also large positive coefficients at lags equal to multiples of 12. This pattern is the momentum seasonality reported by Heston and Sadka (2008). This effect shows up all the way back to lag 120. While these effects have been documented separately in different studies, they can all be captured in one go with a single regression here.

Since the covariates are standardized, we can easily interpret the magnitudes of the coefficients. For example, the "momentum" coefficients in lags $t-2$ to $t-12$ lags sum up to around 0.15%. This means that a positive one-standard deviation move in each of the past 12 months translates into an increase in the predicted return in month t of slightly above 0.15%. Annualized, this would be close to 2%. For comparison, momentum is often analyzed with decile portfolio sorts in which top and bottom decile average returns are differenced. Such a high-minus-low decile portfolio difference represents roughly a three standard deviation dispersion in lagged returns and the average annualized return spread is often in the ballpark of 6.0% depending on the sample period, which is therefore consistent with our estimates here.

As the much smaller magnitude of the coefficients in panel (b) shows, the predictability associated with lagged squared returns appears to be weaker. While the smaller magnitude of coefficients is suggestive of a weaker effect, it is not obvious, though, that the cumulative effect is weaker. Since squared returns are positively autocorrelated, it is more likely that a stock ends up with a series of past return observations consistently in the tails of the distribution than that it ends up with a series of consistently positive or consistently negative returns. The effect of the many small coefficients for squared returns therefore can add up to a non-negligible effect size. That the coefficients are predominantly positive means that stocks with many lagged returns in the tails on both sides of the distribution, especially for longer lags, tend to have higher returns going forward. Put differently, stocks with a history of high lagged volatility tend to have higher returns.

Panel (c) reports the regression coefficients for the 119 lags of returns raised to the third power. There is a tendency for the coefficients to be negative, which indicates that a history of negative tail realizations in returns is associated with higher future returns, but the coefficients are quite small. And unlike for squared returns, returns raised to the third power have little autocorrelation, which means that the cumulative effects are likely quite small relative to those of the simple past returns in panel (a).

The coefficient estimates in Figure 3.1 already hint at two important observations about the properties of asset price data that are relevant to our thinking on how to apply ML methods in this area. First, the signal-to-noise ratio is extremely low. While the return predictability implied by the magnitudes of the coefficient estimates in Figure 3.1 is in line with what has been found in the asset pricing literature elsewhere, the predictable component of returns accounts for only a very small fraction of total return variance. For example, the spread of around 2% in annualized predicted returns associated with a one-standard deviation

TABLE 3.2
Return prediction with a polynomial of lagged returns

Method	Scaling	CV criterion	γ (i)	IS R^2 (ii)	CV R^2 (iii)	CV portfolio return r_p Mean (iv)	S.D. (v)	Sharpe Ratio (vi)
OLS	Equal	n/a	0	5.22	−1.18	4.12	11.60	0.35
Ridge	Equal	R^2	2.25	2.63	0.84	4.20	13.85	0.30
Ridge	Unequal	R^2	1.40	2.69	1.18	4.55	12.47	0.37
Ridge	Unequal	$E[r_p]$	3.11	1.75	0.89	4.58	12.94	0.35
Lasso	Unequal	R^2	0.00028	3.55	0.84	4.25	11.79	0.36

move in lagged 12-month returns is small relative to the typical annualized standard deviation of market-adjusted individual stock returns in
the ballpark of 40% or more. Second, nonlinearities are subtle. While
the inclusion of second and third powers of past returns is a crude
way of dealing with nonlinearities and there are many other types of
potentially relevant nonlinearity, such as interactions between covariates, that we have not explored here, strongly nonlinear effects do not
jump out of the data in an obvious way. To the extent they exist, one
has to look for them with more sophisticated tools in order to find
them.

Table 3.2 presents information on the predictive performance of the
model. All numbers are annualized.[1] The second row presents the estimates for the ridge regression. For comparison, the first row shows the
same statistics for an OLS regression. For now, we focus on the R^2 measures in columns (ii) and (iii). We will discuss the other columns later in
this chapter. Column (ii) shows the in-sample (IS) R^2 in the training data.
The IS R^2 of ridge regression is just about half as big as the IS R^2 of OLS.
However, the cross-validated R^2 from leave-one-year-out cross-validation
(CV) in column (iii) shows that much of the seemingly good in-sample fit
of the OLS regression is in fact coming from overfitting noise: the CV R^2
of OLS takes a negative value of −1.18%. In contrast, the ridge regression
produces a positive CV R^2 of 0.84%. This illustrates that regularization
is important for achieving good predictive performance.

---

[1]The R^2 numbers are annualized by multiplying the monthly numbers by 12, which is a
good approximation as long as the predictable component is a small portion of total return
variance.

These R^2 numbers again highlight the low signal-to-noise ratio in stock return prediction applications. Even though CV R^2 of around 1% are economically substantial—the implied standard deviation of the predictable component of annual returns is about 4%—the predictable component only accounts for a very small part of total return variance.

Since we estimated the hyperparameter γ by maximizing the CV R^2 on the validation folds, the CV R^2 reported in Table 3.2 are not fully out-of-sample. Out-of-sample R^2 on test data sets used neither in model training nor hyperparameter estimation are likely somewhat lower. Later in this chapter, we look at such out-of-sample R^2. But even leaving this issue aside for now, there are questions about the suitability of R^2 measures in predictive performance assessment and as objectives in hyperparameter optimization in an asset pricing application. We look into these issues first.

3.2 PREDICTIVE PERFORMANCE ASSESSMENT

ML applications often focus on minimization of the sum of squared prediction errors. Correspondingly, the sum of squared prediction errors, or functions of it like the R^2, are often used as a predictive performance measure. It may seem natural that minimization of individual stock return prediction error is an appropriate objective in a stock return prediction application, too.

However, it is not obvious that this is the right approach in an asset pricing setting. For example, in a portfolio management application, the ultimate goal often is not to predict returns on individual assets but rather to construct a portfolio that earns a high return relative to its risk out-of-sample. Similarly, when researchers study risk premia or market efficiency, they may be more interested in the risk-return properties of portfolios that aggregate the returns of groups of securities rather than of individual security returns. Methods that yield better predictions of individual security returns, in the sense of a higher predictive R^2, do not necessarily yield better portfolios in terms of standard metrics such as the portfolio's Sharpe ratio. Therefore, the fact that ridge regression in the second row of Table 3.2 produces a higher CV R^2 than an OLS regression does not necessarily mean that a portfolio constructed to exploit the predicted return differences between stocks based on the ridge estimates would perform better on the cross-validation folds than one based on the OLS estimates.

Column (iv) in Table 3.2 illustrates this. This column shows the annualized cross-validated mean return of a portfolio in which individual stocks are weighted by the predicted returns from the estimated regression. In each month t in a validation fold, we weight all stocks with the weights vector

$$\hat{\omega}_{t-1} = \frac{1}{\sum_{i=1}^{N} |\hat{\mu}_{i,t-1}|} \hat{\mu}_{t-1}, \qquad (3.3)$$

which is proportional to the vector of predicted returns $\hat{\mu}_{t-1}$ that we construct from the model estimated on the training folds. Some of the elements of $\hat{\mu}_{t-1}$ are positive—a long position—and some are negative—a short position—and they sum to zero. Scaling by the summation term in the denominator fixes the size of the portfolio to be half a dollar short and half a dollar long. As we did before for the CV R^2, we use leave-one-year-out CV, but this time for the portfolio return $r_{p,t} = \hat{\omega}_{t-1}' r_t$ instead of the R^2. Averaging across time, we obtain the cross-validated mean portfolio return (for penalty parameter tuning, we still stick to maximizing the CV R^2 for now).

As column (iv) shows, the portfolio formed based on ridge regression estimates in the second row achieves a slightly higher CV mean return (4.20%) than the portfolio formed based on OLS regression estimates in the first row (4.12%). But this difference is surprisingly small given how big the difference is in the CV R^2 of these methods. In other words, even though OLS produces a negative predictive R^2 on the cross-validation folds, a portfolio formed based on the OLS regression predictions produces a surprisingly high mean return on the cross-validation folds. Moreover, as column (v) shows, the portfolio based on OLS estimates actually has a lower return standard deviation than the portfolio constructed from ridge regression estimates in the second row. As a consequence, the OLS portfolio earns a higher CV Sharpe ratio (ratio of mean return to standard deviation) than the portfolio based on ridge regression estimates.

To understand this discrepancy between R^2 measures of predictive performance and portfolio performance metrics, we now look into the determinants of these measures in an OLS regression framework. In the next section, we then look at the effects of regularization on these metrics and we ask whether this analysis changes our conclusions about how we should perform hyperparameter tuning.

Consider returns on N stocks that are generated each period as follows:

$$r_t = \mu + \varepsilon_t,$$
$$\mu = Xg. \qquad (3.4)$$

Here r_t is an $N \times 1$ vector of returns in period t, X is an $N \times K$ matrix of predictor variables, and ε_t is a vector of IID shocks with diagonal covariance matrix $\Sigma = I_N \sigma^2$. Since we will focus on cross-sectional differences between stocks, we assume that the returns in r_t are market-adjusted, i.e., the returns are expressed in excess of the returns on some market index.[2]

Now suppose that we have estimated a return-prediction model by regressing average returns, $\bar{r} = \frac{1}{\tau} \sum_{t=1}^{\tau} r_t$, observed from $t = 1$ up to some time $t = \tau$, on the K covariates in X with OLS. This yields predicted returns $\hat{\mu} = X(X'X)^{-1}X'\bar{r}$, which we can decompose as

$$\hat{\mu} = \mu + u, \qquad u = X(X'X)^{-1}X'\bar{\varepsilon}, \tag{3.5}$$

where $\bar{\varepsilon} = \frac{1}{\tau} \sum_{t=1}^{\tau} \varepsilon_t$. Note that $\mathbb{E}[u] = 0$ and $\mathbb{E}[uu'] = \frac{1}{\tau}X(X'X)^{-1}X'\sigma^2$.

We now calculate the OOS R^2 in explaining returns in a validation data set from $t = \tau + 1$ to $t = T$. With total and unexpected average returns in the validation periods of

$$\bar{r}_v = \frac{1}{T-\tau} \sum_{t=\tau+1}^{T} r_t, \qquad \bar{\varepsilon}_v = \frac{1}{T-\tau} \sum_{t=\tau+1}^{T} \varepsilon_t, \tag{3.6}$$

we have $\bar{r}_v = \mu + \bar{\varepsilon}_v$ and the prediction error is $\bar{r}_v - \hat{\mu} = \mu + \bar{\varepsilon}_v - \hat{\mu} = \bar{\varepsilon}_v - u$. Hence we get the OOS R^2

$$
\begin{aligned}
R^2_{OOS} &= 1 - \frac{(\bar{\varepsilon}_v - u)'(\bar{\varepsilon}_v - u)}{(\bar{\varepsilon}_v + \mu)'(\bar{\varepsilon}_v + \mu)} \\
&\approx 1 - \frac{\frac{1}{T-\tau}\sigma^2}{\frac{1}{N}\mu'\mu + \frac{1}{T-\tau}\sigma^2} - \frac{\frac{1}{\tau}\sigma^2}{\frac{1}{N}\mu'\mu + \frac{1}{T-\tau}\sigma^2}.
\end{aligned}
\tag{3.7}
$$

To get the approximation in the second line, we replaced terms like $(1/N)\bar{\varepsilon}_v'u$, $(1/N)u'u$, and $(1/N)\bar{\varepsilon}_v'\bar{\varepsilon}_v$ with their expected values. We will use a similar approximation repeatedly in this chapter.

Looking at (3.7) we see that the OOS R^2 is negatively affected by the third term, which is due to the effect of estimation error. This estimation error component would vanish with large training set size τ. But if τ is sufficiently small, a large estimation error can easily turn the OOS R^2 negative, even though the in-sample R^2 in the training data is always positive.

Rather than the R^2, an investor or a financial economist studying asset prices might be more interested in the return of a portfolio strategy that

---

[2] That X is constant through time—unlike the past-return based predictors in our empirical example—is mostly without loss of generality. This is easiest to see in the case of just one predictor that has been transformed into ranks. In this case, we could re-sort the rows of the predictor vector and r_t each period such the re-sorted predictor vector is exactly the same each period. However, if not only cross-sectional ranks, but also the values of the predictors matter for expected returns such that $\mu_{t-1} = X_{t-1}g$ would be time-varying even after re-sorting the rows of the predictor vector and r_t, the constant X cannot capture this.

exploits cross-sectional differences in expected returns. We consider a portfolio with weights as in (3.3), but with a different scaling factor:

$$\hat{\omega} = \frac{1}{\sqrt{\hat{\mu}'\hat{\mu}}}\hat{\mu}. \tag{3.8}$$

Multiplying estimated expected returns with the ratio $1/\sqrt{\hat{\mu}'\hat{\mu}}$ ensures that the weights have an interpretable scale by fixing the sum of squared weights to 1. For the calculations we do here, this is more convenient than scaling by the sum of absolute portfolio weights, although the portfolio then does not have the interpretation of being exactly half a dollar long and half a dollar short.

Given our assumption here that returns are cross-sectionally uncorrelated, the weights of the mean-variance efficient portfolio—i.e., the portfolio that maximizes the Sharpe ratio of mean return to return standard deviation—are proportional to the vector of expected returns.[3] Therefore, in this special case, the weights $\hat{\omega}$ also represent the (estimated) weights of the mean-variance efficient portfolio.

The portfolio with weights $\hat{\omega}$ earns a per-period return out-of-sample (i.e., for periods $t > \tau$) with expected value and variance of

$$\mathbb{E}[\hat{\omega}'\bar{r}_v|\hat{\omega}] \approx \frac{\mu'\mu}{\sqrt{\mu'\mu + \frac{N}{\tau}\sigma^2}}, \qquad \mathrm{var}(\hat{\omega}'r_v|\hat{\omega}) = \frac{1}{T-\tau}\sigma^2. \tag{3.9}$$

Therefore, the squared Sharpe ratio in the validation period is

$$\frac{(\mathbb{E}[\hat{\omega}'\bar{r}_v|\hat{\omega}])^2}{\mathrm{var}(\hat{\omega}'\bar{r}_v|\hat{\omega})} \approx \left(\frac{T-\tau}{\sigma^2}\right)\frac{(\mu'\mu)^2}{\mu'\mu + \frac{N}{\tau}\sigma^2}. \tag{3.10}$$

In this case, with a diagonal covariance matrix, the squared Sharpe ratio is approximately proportional to the squared expected return of the portfolio in (3.9). So we can focus our discussion for now just on the expected return in (3.9).

Comparing (3.9) with (3.7), we see that, just like the OOS R^2, the expected portfolio return is negatively affected by higher estimation error: the expected return is increasing in the training data set size τ. The reason is that when the training data set is smaller and hence estimation error is

---

[3]The mean-variance efficient portfolio has weights proportional to $\Sigma^{-1}\mu$. If one rescales the weights such that their sum of squares is unity, the weights are $\frac{1}{\sqrt{\mu'\Sigma^{-2}\mu}}\Sigma^{-1}\mu$. This portfolio achieves the maximum Sharpe ratio, i.e., the maximum ratio of expected portfolio excess return to portfolio return standard deviation. We will come back to this special portfolio repeatedly throughout this book.

larger, then $\hat{\mu}$, which is used to construct the portfolio weights according to (3.8), has more noise relative to the signal μ. This leads to larger absolute magnitudes of the elements of $\hat{\mu}$. As a consequence, the portfolio weight denominator $1/\sqrt{\hat{\mu}'\hat{\mu}}$ is larger, which reduces the expected return of the portfolio. The intuition is that for a portfolio where we basically fixed the total exposure to long and short positions, more noise in portfolio weights means that we are using part of this investment capacity to trade on noise rather than on signal.[4]

Based on this analysis so far, one might conclude that since both the R^2 and portfolio mean return are negatively affected by estimation error, the R^2 is a good indicator of portfolio performance. Unfortunately, once we move away from the simple $\Sigma = I_N \sigma^2$ case, this may no longer be true. The portfolio Sharpe ratio in this case depends on the properties of Σ, and R^2 measures are silent about these properties.

But even if we leave the issue of the covariance matrix aside, there are other reasons why R^2 and portfolio performance measures can give conflicting messages. As we saw in (3.2), moving from unregularized OLS to regularized ridge regression had a large effect on the CV R^2, but led to only a minor improvement in the mean portfolio return. This brings up two questions. First, how does regularization affect these predictive performance measures? Second, are off-the-shelf ML approaches to regularization appropriate in an asset pricing application? The objective in penalty hyperparameter tuning is typically to maximize the cross-validated R^2. But improving the R^2 is apparently not necessarily the same thing as improving portfolio performance. For this reason, we first look more closely into the effects of regularization on portfolio performance before we look at consequences of a non-diagonal covariance matrix of returns.

3.3   REGULARIZATION AND INVESTMENT PERFORMANCE

In this section, we examine the effects of regularization on the OOS R^2 and portfolio performance in a validation data set. As before, we use ridge regression as an example, but the lessons we draw from this analysis apply more broadly to other forms of penalized regression like lasso as well.

Suppose that we estimate the parameter vector g in (3.4) with a ridge regression

$$\hat{g} = \left(X'X + \gamma I_K\right)^{-1} X'\bar{r}. \tag{3.11}$$

---

[4]If one instead left the weights unscaled and just equal to $\hat{\mu}$, the expected return would be approximately unaffected by the estimation error, but the variance would be higher, leading to the same detrimental effect on the squared Sharpe ratio.

In this case, regularization takes the form of shrinkage and it kicks in if $\gamma > 0$. Suppose further that $X'X = I_K$, e.g., because we orthonormalized the covariates before running the regression. Then (3.11) simplifies to

$$\hat{g} = \frac{1}{1+\gamma} X'\bar{r}, \tag{3.12}$$

and

$$\hat{\mu} = X\hat{g} = \frac{1}{1+\gamma} XX'\bar{r} = \frac{1}{1+\gamma}\mu + \frac{1}{1+\gamma}u, \tag{3.13}$$

where

$$u = XX'\bar{\varepsilon}. \tag{3.14}$$

The R^2 in the validation data is now a modified version of (3.7) because of the shrinkage effects. We obtain

$$R_{OOS}^2 \approx 1 - \frac{\frac{1}{T-\tau}\sigma^2}{\frac{1}{N}\mu'\mu + \frac{1}{T-\tau}\sigma^2} - \left(\frac{\gamma^2}{(1+\gamma)^2}\right)\frac{\frac{1}{N}\mu'\mu}{\frac{1}{N}\mu'\mu + \frac{1}{T-\tau}\sigma^2}$$

$$- \left(\frac{1}{(1+\gamma)^2}\right)\frac{\frac{1}{\tau}\sigma^2}{\frac{1}{N}\mu'\mu + \frac{1}{T-\tau}\sigma^2}. \tag{3.15}$$

We can use this expression to evaluate the effects of shrinkage on the OOS R^2. The last term is due to estimation error and it subtracts from the R^2. The shrinkage induced by $\gamma > 0$ reduces the magnitude of this term. This raises the OOS R^2. But shrinkage also introduces the second term because it biases $\hat{\mu}$ away from μ. Greater shrinkage increases the magnitude of this term, which in turn reduces the OOS R^2. Whether the combined effect of shrinkage raises or lowers R_{OOS}^2 depends on the magnitudes of γ, $\frac{1}{N}\mu'\mu$, and $\frac{1}{\tau}\sigma^2$. The larger the noise variance $\frac{1}{\tau}\sigma^2$ relative to the signal variance $\frac{1}{N}\mu'\mu$, the greater the R_{OOS}^2-maximizing γ.

But investors do not necessarily care about the OOS R^2 directly. How would such scaling affect the out-of-sample performance of a portfolio strategy formed based on the estimates $\hat{\mu}$ as in (3.8)? It turns out that shrinking estimates by constant factor $\frac{1}{1+\gamma}$ in (3.13) leaves the weights $\hat{\omega} = \frac{1}{\sqrt{\hat{\mu}'\hat{\mu}}}\hat{\mu}$ unchanged! As a consequence, expected returns, variance, and squared Sharpe ratio will remain unchanged as well.[5] This is an important lesson: improvement of the OOS R^2 is not a guarantee that OOS portfolio performance measures improve, too.

[5] If one used unscaled weights instead, $\hat{\omega} = \hat{\mu}$, the expected return would fall, and the portfolio return standard deviation would fall by the same factor, leaving the squared Sharpe ratio unchanged.

That improvement in OOS R^2 does not necessarily translate into improved portfolio performance is true even in this simplified setting with uncorrelated regression residuals. Therefore, this disconnect between OOS R^2 and portfolio performance is not simply due a consequence of the OOS R^2's neglect of prediction error covariances in summarizing the predictive performance. In fact, we would get the same result with a general covariance matrix Σ. In this case, plug-in estimates of mean-variance efficient portfolio weights would be $\hat{\omega} = \frac{1}{\sqrt{\hat{\mu}'\Sigma^{-2}\hat{\mu}}}\Sigma^{-1}\hat{\mu}$. It is easy to see that the effects of shrinking $\hat{\mu}$ by a scalar factor would cancel out in these weights, leaving no effect on portfolio performance measures.

This can help us understand why moving from OLS to ridge regression in Table 3.2 had a big effect on the CV R^2, but not on portfolio performance measures. We used standardized covariates in these regressions, which means that the covariates do not have any heterogeneity in their cross-sectional dispersion. And the covariates are not highly correlated with each other. This means the empirical setting in Table 3.2 is such that $X'X$ is close to proportional to the identity matrix—just like in our analysis in this section so far. In this case, ridge regression shrinks all coefficients about equally. This helps the R^2, but not portfolio mean returns and the Sharpe ratio. For shrinkage to have an effect on portfolio performance metrics, shrinkage has to operate in a more subtle way than by just shrinking all elements of the estimated expected return vector by a constant factor. In the case we considered so far, with $X'X = I_K$, shrinkage scales back not only the estimation error in the weights but also, to the same degree, the expected return signal component in weights.

For shrinkage to potentially improve portfolio performance, it has to be the case that $X'X$ is not proportional to an identity matrix. Consider, for example, the case where

$$X = Q_K \Lambda_K^{\frac{1}{2}} \tag{3.16}$$

for some $N \times K$ matrix Q_K and a diagonal matrix Λ_K with diagonal elements λ_j. To keep notation simple, we still assume that predictors have been orthogonalized, but without scaling them to have equal cross-sectional variances. This means here that the columns of Q_K are orthonormal, i.e., $Q_K'Q_K = I_K$, but $X'X = \Lambda_K$, so the diagonal elements of Λ_K determine the cross-sectional dispersion of the covariates. Unlike in the $X'X = I_K$ case, we can now have covariates that differ in terms of their cross-sectional dispersion.

In this case, OLS would yield estimates $\hat{g}_{OLS} = \Lambda_K^{-\frac{1}{2}}Q_K'\bar{r}$ and predicted returns $\hat{\mu}_{OLS} = X\hat{g}_{OLS}$. The predicted returns from a ridge regression are

$$\hat{\mu} = X \left(\Lambda_K + \gamma I_K \right)^{-1} \Lambda_K^{\frac{1}{2}} Q_K' \bar{r}$$

$$= X \left(I_K + \gamma \Lambda_K^{-1} \right)^{-1} \hat{g}_{OLS}. \qquad (3.17)$$

Comparing with $\hat{\mu}_{OLS}$, we can see that ridge regression, with $\gamma > 0$, now applies shrinkage to different degrees depending on the λ_j associated with column j of Q_K. Predictors with low λ_j, which means predictors that have little cross-sectional dispersion, have large entries in the Λ_K^{-1} matrix, which means that their coefficients get shrunk more than those of predictors with high λ_j. Since they have little cross-sectional dispersion, the effects of these low-λ_j predictors on expected returns are difficult to estimate. Therefore, it may be beneficial to downweight this covariate because it makes a large contribution to estimation error. If the benefits from reduced estimation error outweigh the costs of downweighting the expected return signal in this covariate, shrinkage can improve portfolio performance.

Since shrinkage in this case is not simply scaling all coefficients by the same scalar, it is possible that the Sharpe ratio in the validation period could be improved through shrinkage. With $\Sigma = I_N \sigma^2$ and portfolio weights $\hat{\omega} = \frac{1}{\sqrt{\hat{\mu}'\hat{\mu}}} \hat{\mu}$, we get expected return and variance of

$$\mathbb{E}[\hat{w}'\bar{r}_v | \hat{w}] \approx \frac{g' \Lambda_K \left(I_K + \gamma \Lambda_K^{-1} \right)^{-1} g}{\sqrt{g' \Lambda_K \left(I_K + \gamma \Lambda_K^{-1} \right)^{-2} g + \frac{1}{\tau} \sigma^2 \, \mathrm{tr} \left[\left(I_K + \gamma \Lambda_K^{-1} \right)^{-2} \right]}},$$

$$\mathrm{var}(\hat{w}'\bar{r}_v | \hat{w}) = \frac{1}{T - \tau} \sigma^2. \qquad (3.18)$$

We can rewrite the expected return as

$$\mathbb{E}[\hat{w}'\bar{r}_v | \hat{w}] \approx \frac{\sum_{j=1}^{K} \frac{g_j^2 \lambda_j}{1 + \gamma \lambda_j^{-1}}}{\sqrt{\sum_{j=1}^{K} \frac{g_j^2 \lambda_j}{(1 + \gamma \lambda_j^{-1})^2} + \frac{1}{\tau} \sigma^2 \sum_{j=1}^{K} \frac{1}{(1 + \gamma \lambda_j^{-1})^2}}}. \qquad (3.19)$$

The second term in the denominator reflects the effect of estimation error. Shrinkage with $\gamma > 0$ shrinks the magnitude of this term. However, it also shrinks the term in the numerator. Which effect dominates depends on the properties of g and Λ_K. Increasing γ leads to a large reduction in the estimator error term in the denominator if there are some λ_j that are very small. This is due to the fact that if some λ_j are small, ridge regression shrinks these components the most, which reduces estimation error. The cost of this increased shrinkage is the forgone return prediction power as captured by the numerator. But this cost is small if $g_j^2 \lambda_j$, i.e., the predictable return variation associated with this covariate, is not high. In this case, the relatively small cost of forgone predictive power is worth paying given the benefit from reducing estimation error.

Since the variance of the portfolio return is unaffected by shrinkage, any improvement in the expected return would also translate into an improvement in the Sharpe ratio. Hence, for shrinkage to improve portfolio performance relative to unregularized OLS regressions in a setting with cross-sectionally homoskedastic and uncorrelated returns, as well as orthogonalized covariates, the covariates must differ in their cross sectional dispersion. Only then will ridge regression shrink the coefficients of different covariates to different degrees, which is required for shrinkage to have an effect on portfolio performance.

More generally, shrinkage can improve portfolio performance if there is heterogeneity in the covariates' relative contribution to expected return and to estimation error. Heterogeneity in contributions to risk is another relevant dimension that we have not considered yet. Shrinkage must affect undesirable contributions (estimation error, risk) more than desirable ones (expected returns).

A somewhat similar conclusion applies for the lasso. But in the lasso case, heterogeneity in the magnitudes of the true g_j coefficients can be an additional reason why regularization can affect portfolio performance. Even if there are no differences in the cross-sectional dispersion of the covariates, the lasso would set to zero coefficients whose OLS estimates are close to zero (recall our discussion of lasso shrinkage in section 2.2.1). Therefore, heterogeneity in the g_j could also induce heterogeneous shrinkage effects that improve portfolio performance.

Returning to the ridge regression case, the results of our analysis so far still do not give us much guidance. What does it really mean for some covariates to have lower cross-sectional dispersion than others? In a typical asset pricing application, we could rescale the predictors in arbitrary ways. For example, predictors are often expressed as portfolio ranks, or cross-sectionally standardized to unit standard deviation. This is precisely what we have done in the return prediction regressions in Table 3.2. With such standardization, the cross-sectional dispersion of each predictor is identical. If predictors are also uncorrelated cross-sectionally, ridge regression shrinks all coefficients equally, with no effect on portfolio Sharpe ratios. But why this type of scaling and not a different one?

Standard ridge and lasso statistical packages often standardize variables before estimation by default. Our discussion here makes clear that this is not an innocuous data preprocessing step because it affects what is being shrunk! If the covariate second moment matrix is diagonal, standardizing the covariates guarantees that there will be no effect on portfolio performance metrics compared with OLS! Standardizing therefore has a substantive effect on the estimation outcomes.

More generally, the outcomes of the ridge regression prediction and portfolio formation exercises are not invariant to rescaling covariates: we can redefine covariates and coefficients in (3.16), without changing the assets' expected returns, in a way that changes the ridge regression outcomes. For example, continuing with our example from above, if we redefine the regression coefficients as $\Lambda_K^{\frac{1}{2}} g$ and the covariates as $X\Lambda_K^{-\frac{1}{2}} = Q_K$, ridge regression yields

$$\hat{\mu} = Q_K (I_K + \gamma I_K)^{-1} Q_K' \bar{r} = \frac{1}{1+\gamma} X \hat{g}_{OLS}, \qquad (3.20)$$

where $\hat{g}_{OLS} = \Lambda_K^{-\frac{1}{2}} Q_K' \bar{r}$ is the OLS estimator from the regression of $\bar{r}$ on the original covariates X. Thus, we are back to having a constant shrinkage factor that affects all elements of $\hat{\mu}$ equally! In this case, changing γ has no effect on the mean return and Sharpe ratio of the portfolio formed based on $\hat{\mu}$.

So if arbitrary rescaling of covariates can affect the properties of ridge regression shrinkage, how should we rescale the covariates? This is one of the places where we need to bring in prior knowledge about the properties of the data that we are training the model on. If we have prior reasons to think that some covariates might be less important than others, and might just contribute a lot to estimation error rather than return prediction signal, then we could rescale such that these likely less important covariates have a lower cross-sectional dispersion.

For this purpose, it is useful to recall from Section 2.4 the interpretation of ridge regression as a Bayesian regression with normal prior for the regression coefficients. Ridge regression arises as a special case of the Bayesian regression if the prior covariance matrix and residual covariance matrix are proportional to the identity matrix. Put differently, if we apply standard ridge regression, we are implicitly expressing the prior belief that nature draws each element of g from the same distribution. In a ridge regression, we should therefore rescale covariates in such a way that this implicit assumption is plausible. In other words, based on what we know about the prediction problem and the data, it should be plausible that each covariate could get a coefficient of roughly equal magnitude. If some covariates are less important in terms of their contribution to predictable returns according to our prior beliefs, then they should be scaled to have lower cross-sectional dispersion so it is still plausible that they get roughly similar regression coefficient magnitudes as the other more important covariates.

For example, in our return prediction example, we might be skeptical about the presence of nonlinearities in the relationships between past stock returns and future stock returns. This would lead us to rescale the second- and third-order terms in (3.2) to have lower cross-sectional standard deviation than the first-order terms. To illustrate the effects of such rescaling, we add another rescaling step in our empirical example: after standardizing the covariates, we divide the squared return covariates by 2, and the third-order covariates by 4. There is of course some arbitrariness in the choice of these scaling factors, but the purpose here is merely to illustrate that such rescaling can affect predictive performance.

The third row of Table 3.2—labelled "unequal" to highlight the different type of scaling of the covariates—presents the results. One change compared with the second row in the table is the substantially lower value of the estimated penalty parameter γ. Once the covariates are rescaled to have unequal cross-sectional standard deviations, we need less shrinkage to maximize the CV R^2. As a consequence, even the in-sample R^2 rises slightly from 2.63% in the second row to 2.69% in the third. More importantly, the CV R^2 rises by more than a third from 0.84% to 1.18% and portfolio performance measures improve: the mean return rises from 4.20% to 4.55% and the Sharpe ratio from 0.30 to 0.37. Evidently, the prior belief that the second- and third-order terms are less important for return prediction seems to have some validity in the data.

Finally, since we now understand that there is a clear difference between R^2 measures of predictive performance and portfolio performance in the validation periods, it is natural to ask why we even use the R^2 as an objective for hyperparameter tuning. If we want to maximize portfolio performance measures, why not target them directly in our hyperparameter tuning? The fourth row in Table 3.2 shows what happens when we do this in our return prediction example, sticking to the unequal scaling that downscales the second- and third-order terms. In this version of the ridge regression, we tune the penalty parameter to maximize the mean return of the portfolio in the validation folds, not the R^2. The consequences are interesting. The estimated γ of 3.11 is much higher than in the third row where we picked γ to maximize the CV R^2. The IS and CV R^2 are therefore both substantially lower than in the third row. Nevertheless, the portfolio mean return (4.58% vs. 4.55%) is slightly higher. The Sharpe ratio (0.35 vs. 0.37) is slightly lower, though. But if one wanted to maximize the Sharpe ratio, one could target it directly instead of the mean return in the hyperparameter tuning. Broadly, these results suggest that the gains from tweaking the penalty parameters by directly targeting portfolio performance instead of R^2 are quite limited, at least in this specific setting. But they also illustrate once more that R^2 measures can be quite misleading as indicators of portfolio performance.

The bottom line conclusion from this section is that the effects of regularization on R^2 and portfolio performance in validation data are sensitive to the scaling of covariates. For regularization to be effective, we need to bring in some prior knowledge about the likely relative importance of different covariates in the prediction task. This raises the question of how we might come up with prior beliefs that can help us scale covariates appropriately to make regularization effective. As the next section shows, financial economics suggests links between covariances and expected returns, and these links can help us pin down how we should regularize.

3.4   Links between Expected Returns and Covariances

The Bayesian regression framework we discussed in Section 2.4 allows us to tackle the question of covariate scaling by showing how economic links between expected returns and covariances relate to regularization. Recall that for a cross-sectional regression model $\bar{r} = Xg + \bar{e}$ with a prior $g \sim \mathcal{N}(0, \Sigma_g)$, where $\bar{r}$ and $\bar{e}$ are averages of r_t and e_t from a sample of size τ, and $\Sigma = \text{var}(e_t)$, we get the posterior mean

$$\hat{g} = \left(X'\Sigma^{-1}X + \frac{1}{\tau}\Sigma_g^{-1} \right)^{-1} X'\Sigma^{-1}\bar{r}. \tag{3.21}$$

Within this framework, we now look for a specification of X and prior beliefs about g that are economically sensible. For this purpose, we also need a more realistic specification of the covariance matrix. The assumption that $\Sigma = I_N\sigma^2$ that we worked with above is sometimes useful for illustration, but not a realistic property of asset returns. Here we let Σ have a general form. As before, we still assume that Σ is known and does not need to be estimated.

Economic reasoning suggests that covariates that predict returns should be related to stock return covariances. Specifically, the link to the covariance matrix should be such that if a long-short portfolio formed based on the values of a covariate produces a substantial mean return, it should also have substantial return volatility. For example, if small firm size predicts high returns, then a portfolio that takes a long position in small stocks and a short position in large stocks should have substantial volatility. This requires covariance risk exposure in the sense that small stocks co-move with each other more than with large stocks and large stocks co-move with each other more than with small stocks. This within-group comovement prevents risk from diversifying away with the consequence that a long-short portfolio then has relatively high return variance. As Kozak, Nagel, and Santosh (2018) discuss, such links between mean returns and covariances are predicted by a wide range of asset pricing models, including ones with rational investors and ones that include investors whose asset demand is driven by sentiment or behavioral biases. If such links between expected returns and covariances were absent, economically implausible near-arbitrage opportunities would exist.

To arrive at a particularly transparent result, we specify this link between return-predicting covariates and covariances through the somewhat stark assumption that the K vectors of covariates used to predict returns are equal to K eigenvectors of Σ. Let $\Sigma = Q\Lambda Q'$ be the eigendecomposition of Σ and let Q_K be a selection of K columns of the orthogonal matrix Q. We then assume that $X = Q_K$, which implies $X'X = I_K$. The assumption that covariates are exactly equal to the eigenvectors is, of course, a strong assumption, but it will give us a particularly clear result.

Since the portfolio weights are based on eigenvectors, or principal components, of the return covariance matrix, we label them principal component (PC) portfolios. The PC portfolios have expected returns and variance

$$\mathbb{E}[Q_K'r_t] = g, \qquad \text{var}(Q_K'r_t) = \Lambda_K, \qquad (3.22)$$

where Λ_K is a diagonal matrix with the K eigenvalues corresponding to the K eigenvectors in Q_K on its diagonal.

We are now in a position to specify economically motivated prior beliefs about g. For this purpose, it is useful to note that the Sharpe Ratios associated with each of these K PC portfolio returns, $r_p = Q_K'r_t$, are $\Lambda_K^{-1/2}g$. An assumption about these Sharpe ratios that has some economic plausibility—more on this in the next chapter—is that high Sharpe ratios are concentrated among PC portfolios that have relatively high variance. Here this would mean that the Sharpe ratio vector $\Lambda_K^{-1/2}g$ is likely to take on greater magnitudes for those elements j associated with high λ_j. Prior beliefs

$$g \sim \mathcal{N}(0, \gamma^{-1}\Lambda_K^2), \qquad 0 < \gamma < 1, \qquad (3.23)$$

would be consistent with this reasoning because they imply prior beliefs about the Sharpe ratio vector $\Lambda_K^{-1/2}g \sim \mathcal{N}(0, \gamma^{-1}\Lambda_K)$. This prior distribution for the Sharpe ratio vector allows for greater magnitude (positive or negative) of Sharpe ratios for those portfolios returns in $r_p = Q_K'r_t$ that are based on columns of Q_K (or X) associated with high λ_j.

Proceeding with this assumption, the hyperparameter γ now has an economic interpretation as controlling the expected squared Sharpe ratio under prior beliefs. To see this, note that the maximum squared Sharpe ratio attainable from the assets is $g'Q'_K \Sigma^{-1} Q_K g$. Taking expectations under the prior distribution, we get

$$\mathbb{E}[g'Q'_K \Sigma^{-1} Q_K g] = \mathbb{E}[g' \Lambda_K^{-1} g] = \frac{1}{\gamma} \operatorname{tr}(\Lambda_K). \qquad (3.24)$$

This expression shows that the prior parameter γ controls the maximum squared Sharpe ratio expected under the prior beliefs. If we choose a high γ in the prior (3.23) we are implicitly expressing the view that the magnitude of Sharpe ratio attainable from these assets is likely to be relatively small. Under this prior view, estimates of Sharpe ratios in empirical data are regarded as likely upward biased because of overfitted noise. Accordingly, these empirical Sharpe ratios get shrunk toward zero in a Bayesian regression. Furthermore, given a value for γ, a higher maximum squared Sharpe ratio is expected if the K PC portfolios have high return variances and hence $\operatorname{tr}(\Lambda_K)$ is high.

Given the prior beliefs in (3.23), the Bayesian regression of $\bar{r}$ on $X = Q_K$ in (3.21) becomes

$$\hat{g} = \left(\Lambda_K^{-1} + \frac{\gamma}{\tau} \Lambda_K^{-2} \right)^{-1} \Lambda_K^{-1} Q'_K \bar{r}$$

$$= \left(I_K + \frac{\gamma}{\tau} \Lambda_K^{-1} \right)^{-1} Q'_K \bar{r}, \qquad (3.25)$$

where $Q'_K \bar{r}$ is the vector of OLS estimates. Recall from (3.22) that we can interpret $\hat{g}$ here as the predicted returns of the PC portfolios. These predicted returns are shrunk toward zero from the OLS estimates. Shrinkage is particularly strong for PC portfolios that have low variance and hence small entries in Λ_K, and big entries in Λ_K^{-1}, corresponding to these portfolios. This type of shrinkage expresses the prior beliefs that these low-variance portfolios are unlikely to be the source of high Sharpe ratios.

The assumptions here that the covariates are exactly equal to K eigenvectors of Σ is not quite realistic. We would expect some relationship between return predictors and eigenvectors of the covariance matrix (again, so that a long-short portfolio formed based on the values of a covariate loads up on covariance risk), but the relationship is unlikely to be as tight as we assumed here. Even so, the analysis in this transparent special case illustrates how one can use the Bayesian approach to bring economic priors into the analysis and give an economic interpretation to shrinkage parameters.

By setting up the regression in a Bayesian framework, we have also removed the arbitrariness of covariate scaling. If we rescaled covariates here, then to keep the prior beliefs about $\mu = Xg$ unchanged, we would have to change the prior about g accordingly. For example, if we divide covariate j by a constant c, we have to multiply the corresponding coefficient g_j in our prior by c, which means multiplying its variance in the prior distribution by c^2. As a consequence, the posterior mean of μ would remain invariant to such rescaling. We revisit these questions again in the next chapter within a more general framework. This framework will allow us to specify prior beliefs in an empirically plausible way.

3.5 RETURN COVARIANCES AND PORTFOLIO AGGREGATION

Covariances of prediction errors play a much bigger role in asset pricing than in typical ML applications. If our aim is to use a return prediction model to form a portfolio with high return relative to the level of risk, the covariance matrix of the unpredictable component of returns plays an important role.

While we have assumed so far that the covariance matrix is known, in practice it must be estimated. This introduces an additional layer of estimation errors that can lead to substantial problems in portfolio construction. In the extreme case, if one wanted to work with thousands individual stocks, finding the mean-variance efficient combination of these stocks would require an estimate of a huge covariance matrix with millions of elements. Estimating this covariance matrix would be difficult without imposing substantial constraints on its functional form or some form of shrinkage estimation applied to the covariance matrix. Moreover, typical individual stock return data sets are unbalanced panels that may be difficult to work with for the purpose of covariance matrix estimation. Finally, in data sets spanning many years or decades, an individual stock's covariance properties are likely to change over time as the firm's characteristics change.

For this reason, it can make sense to first aggregate stocks into portfolios based on the covariates of the return prediction model. If the characteristics that we use to form portfolios are related to stocks' covariance exposures, the covariances of portfolios could be much more stable than covariances of individual stocks. And portfolio aggregation should help with covariance matrix estimation, at least as long as the number of covariates is smaller than the number of assets, i.e., $K < N$.

What would be ideal conditions under which we can aggregate into these portfolios, and hence get these benefits, without negatively affecting the investment opportunities in terms of the maximum squared Sharpe ratio? To make this more concrete, assume again, as earlier in (3.4), that returns are generated as $r = Xg + \varepsilon$, with a predictable component $\mu = Xg$. Consider covariate-weighted portfolios with realized return $r_p = X'r$, expected return $\mu_p = X'\mu = X'Xg$, and return covariance matrix $\Sigma_p = X'\Sigma X$. What are the conditions on the relationship between the covariates in X and asset return covariances such that the maximum squared Sharpe ratio available from individual assets is equal to the maximum squared Sharpe ratio available from the aggregated portfolios?

Hence, we are looking for conditions under which $\mu'\Sigma^{-1}\mu = \mu'_p\Sigma_p^{-1}\mu_p$, i.e.,

$$g'X'\Sigma^{-1}Xg = g'X'X\left(X'\Sigma X\right)^{-1}X'Xg. \qquad (3.26)$$

A necessary and sufficient condition for this equality to hold (Amemiya (1985), Theorem 6.1.1) is that the covariance matrix takes the form

$$\Sigma = X\Psi X' + U\Phi U' + \sigma^2 I_N, \qquad (3.27)$$

for some conformable matrices Ψ, Φ, and a matrix U such that $U'X = 0$. If and only if the covariance matrix is of this form, then aggregation by X does not lead to a loss of any investment opportunities for a mean-variance investor. Intuitively, for the covariance matrix to take this form requires that the covariates in X capture not only the cross-sectional variation in expected returns, but also the assets' loadings on factors that generate systematic time-series variation in returns (as captured by the first term in (3.27)) such that the assets' loadings U on any remaining systematic factors (as captured by the second term in (3.27)) are orthogonal to X. Any remaining risk not accounted for by these two types of systematic factors must be purely idiosyncratic (the third term in (3.27)).

That the condition (3.27) approximately holds would not be unreasonable in applications with large numbers of covariates in X. Suppose, for example, that Σ has an L-factor structure $\Sigma = G\Omega G' + \sigma^2 I_N$, where G is an $N \times L$ factor loading matrix and Ω is nonsingular. For typical data sets of stock returns, the vast share of stock return covariances are attributable to a small number of factors, say $L \leq 20$. If the X matrix contains many characteristics that are informative about the stocks' factor loadings, then it may be the case that G is approximately spanned by X, i.e., $G \approx XB$ for some matrix B. In this case, $\Sigma \approx XB\Omega B'X' + \sigma^2 I_N$, i.e., we have, approximately, a special case of (3.27). In other words, if there is a limited number of major sources of covariances in individual asset returns and we use a relatively large number of characteristics that tend to be related to the assets' loadings on the major sources of covariances, the deterioration in investment opportunities due to portfolio aggregation may be small.

Moreover, these results above are stated in terms of the population moments. They presume that an investor would know exactly the expected returns and covariances of the asset returns. If we now also take into account the fact that these moments must be estimated in practice, aggregation to portfolios brings benefits by making estimation of the covariance matrix feasible and less prone to estimation error—at least as long as the number of covariates, and hence the number of portfolios, is smaller than the number of individual assets.

In the next chapter, we proceed with this portfolio aggregation approach. This allows us to implement Bayesian regression methods, taking into account the covariance matrix, and to make further progress in tying prior beliefs to economic considerations.

3.6   Nonlinearity

Nonlinearities play a big role in many ML applications. Neural networks and tree-based methods are methods of choice in many settings because of their ability to learn complex nonlinear patterns in the data. In contrast, in our simple past return-based return prediction example earlier in this chapter, the inclusion of second- and third-order terms does not contribute much to return predictability. Adjusting the covariate scaling so that ridge regression downweights these nonlinear terms (when going from the third to the fourth row in Table 3.2) actually improves the predictive performance of the model. This simple empirical example of course does not prove that nonlinearities are unimportant in return prediction. But it is at least suggestive that nonlinearities do not jump out from asset price data as obviously as they do in many ML applications in other fields.

Interactions between covariates, rather than additive nonlinearity of individual predictors, are perhaps a more plausible source of nonlinearities in return prediction models. For example, it seems likely that some return predictability patterns could be stronger among smaller, illiquid stocks. This is an interaction effect that cannot be captured with a model in which predictors enter only additively. Similarly, there could be variables that indicate whether a stock is particularly strongly exposed to investor sentiment or to macroeconomic risks in ways that affect future returns. These would again be interaction effects.

Empirical evidence is emerging that such interactions may be relevant. Chen, Pelger, and Zhu (2019) estimate a deep neural network in which a variety of firm characteristics serve as predictors of returns and second moments. They find that to the extent nonlinearities are present, they show up as interactions between covariates. Similarly, studying neural networks and regression trees, Gu, Kelly, and Xiu (2020a) find that nonlinearities predominantly appear in the form of interactions, not as additive nonlinearities of individual predictors. Bryzgalova,

Pelger, and Zhu (2019) investigate tree-based portfolios in which the universe of stocks is split sequentially in several steps by firm characteristics. This approach allows for higher-order interaction effects between characteristics and they show that these interactions are important for capturing differences in risk and return between stocks. Moritz and Zimmermann (2016) find that interaction effects show up even with the set of predictors restricted, as in the empirical example earlier in this chapter, to functions of stocks' own past returns. They present evidence that interactions between different lags of past returns add predictive power in return prediction. In line with the evidence from these papers highlighting the role of interactions, the empirical analysis presented in the next chapter will allow for interactions between firm characteristics.

3.7 SPARSITY

Methods that induce sparsity have been successful in many ML applications. In these applications, a selection of a small number of covariates tends to be sufficient to obtain good, robust predictive performance. It is quite natural that asset pricing researchers have followed this lead. Many efforts to bring ML methods into asset pricing have focused on lasso-type methods that allow for sparsity, including Chinco, Clark-Joseph, and Ye (2019), DeMiguel, Martin-Utrera, Nogales, and Uppal (2019), Feng, Giglio, and Xiu (2020), and Freyberger, Neuhierl, and Weber (2020). But, as we already discussed at the beginning of this chapter, it is not obvious that sparsity-inducing priors have much justification in asset pricing applications.

The last row of Table 3.2 shows what we get when we apply a lasso regression, as in (2.8), to our past returns-based prediction example. Specifically, we apply it to the scaled version in which the magnitudes of the second- and third-order covariates, after standardization, are scaled down by a factor of 2 and 4, respectively. This is the same scaling that we used in the ridge regressions in rows three and four of this table. The optimal penalty takes a much lower value for lasso than for ridge regression because the regression coefficient estimates are all much smaller than 1 in absolute magnitude and so the sum of absolute coefficients in the lasso penalty is much bigger than the sum of squared coefficients in the ridge penalty. Roughly speaking, the same degree of regularization then happens with a lower value of the penalty hyperparameter. In terms of fit, the IS R^2 of 3.55% is higher than for the ridge regression in the third row. In contrast, predictive performance according to the CV R^2 is quite a bit worse for lasso (0.84% vs. 1.18%). Thus, in terms of the predictive

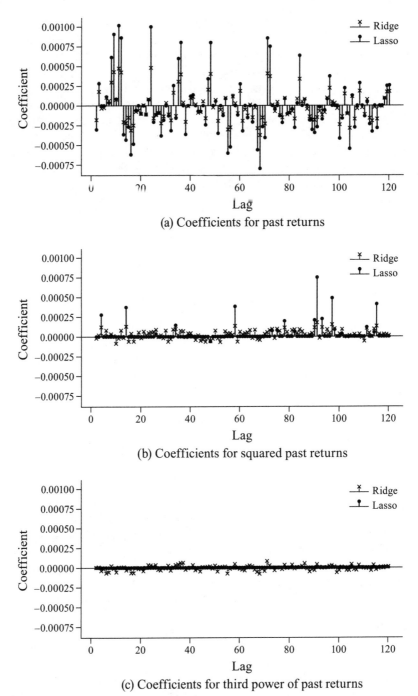

(a) Coefficients for past returns

(b) Coefficients for squared past returns

(c) Coefficients for third power of past returns

Figure 3.2. Comparison of lasso and ridge regression coefficient estimates

performance criterion that is maximized by the procedure, lasso does worse than ridge regression.

Looking at the portfolio performance measures in Table 3.2, lasso does somewhat worse than ridge in terms of the mean return, but the standard deviation of the portfolio return is lower as well, and so the Sharpe ratio ends up slightly higher. This illustrates again that conclusions based on R^2 and portfolio performance measures can diverge substantially. While lasso looks at least comparable to ridge in terms of Sharpe ratio, the sparsity induced by lasso does not yield an edge in performance. Overall, the results add a small piece of evidence that sparsity is not as helpful for predictive performance in asset pricing as it can be in many other ML applications.

Figure 3.2 compares the individual regression coefficients estimated by lasso (marked with a dot) with those from the ridge regression (marked with a cross) with similarly scaled covariates in the third row of Table 3.2. Overall, the estimates reveal the general tendency of lasso to shrink coefficients less than ridge, unless they are shrunk all the way to zero. For the first-order terms in panel (a), only very few of them are set to zero. This again ties in well with our discussion that in return prediction exercises like this one, we do not have strong a priori reasons to expect sparsity.

In contrast, from the estimates shown in panels (b) and (c) we can see that most of the coefficients that have been set to zero are all coefficients for second- and third-order terms. Ridge regression estimates of these coefficients are close to zero, but lasso sets many of them to exactly zero. Thus, lasso almost completely discards the nonlinear terms from the model. This is another illustration of the fact that in settings like this one, with low signal-to-noise ratio and essentially no a priori reason to expect particular types of additive nonlinearities, the data do not strongly call for specifications that allow individual covariates to enter nonlinearly. For predictive performance it does not make much difference, however, whether one sets the coefficients of the second- and third-order terms to exactly zero or leaves them at a magnitude close to zero.

A preliminary conclusion from this analysis is that one should not take it for granted that sparsity is helpful for predictive performance in asset pricing. We take up this issue of sparsity again in the next chapter.

3.8 STRUCTURAL CHANGE

One of the perhaps biggest differences between asset pricing and many common ML applications is that the data-generating process in financial markets is likely undergoing continuous structural change. There are multiple reasons for these changes. First, the economy overall is

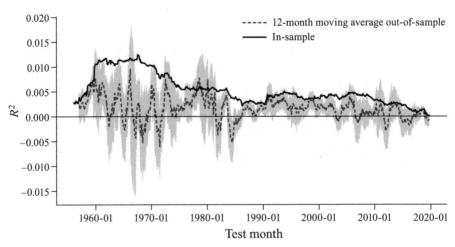

Figure 3.3. Rolling forward out-of-sample prediction R^2

undergoing structural change. Given that technology, regulation, and the institutional environment have changed very much during the past decades, it would be surprising if the relationship between firm characteristics and future stock returns had stayed the same. Second, as we already discussed at the beginning of this chapter, investors learn from data. Past evidence of return predictability may have induced them to alter their trading strategies in a way that destroyed earlier patterns of return predictability. Predictability that shows up historical data therefore might not repeat in the same way in future data.

In the ML literature, the structural change problem is known as *concept drift*. To address the problem, various methods have been developed to allow parameters to adapt over time to the structural changes in the data. For instance, this can be done with a weighting scheme that gives more weight to recent data in the training of an algorithm. A particularly simple example is a rolling window approach where data prior to a certain vintage is completely discarded. Exponential weighting of past data is an alternative that gradually downweights old data. While such methods exist, there has been little work so far on bringing such methods into asset pricing applications of ML and to figure out which ones work best.

Figure 3.3 applies the simple rolling window approach to the past-returns based prediction example in Figure 3.1. Here the ridge regression with first-, second-, and third-order terms of the predictors is estimated within 20-year rolling windows. The penalty hyperparameter is tuned using within-window leave-one-year-out CV. For this exercise, we use the entire CRSP data set starting in 1926, subject to the same NYSE size cutoff and minimum lagged price requirement as in Figure 3.1. Based on the coefficient estimates from each window, we then forecast returns in the first month after the estimation window ends. Given the 20-year estimation window and the up to 10-year lag of the predictors, the first month in which we have a prediction is January 1956, 30 years after the start of the CRSP database. We record the OOS R^2 in this month and then move the 20-year window forward by one month to repeat the process.

Figure 3.3 plots the time series of these OOS R^2 in the form of a 12-month moving average. For comparison, we also show, for each month t, the IS R^2 from the estimation window ending in month t. Several facts in this figure are noteworthy. First, the OOS R^2 is almost everywhere smaller than the IS R^2. Thus, even though regularization in ridge regression should help prevent overfitting, the cross-validated IS R^2 still seems to be an upward biased estimate of the OOS R^2. Part of the reason could be that CV is used to tune the penalty hyperparameter. In this sense, the CV R^2 may still be prone to overfitting because we picked the penalty to minimize it. But very likely, structural change also accounts for a substantial part of the R^2-decay from IS to OOS. Some of the predictive relationships between covariates and future returns that exist in past data simply do not carry over into future data. Consistent with such a structural change, both the IS and OOS R^2 have a tendency to decline toward zero over time. In the last 10–15 years of the sample, the average OOS R^2 is close to zero.

Rather than simple rolling-window estimation, an approach that gradually downweights observations in the more distant past may perform better in tracking changing parameters. For example, exponential weighting is implied by the steady-state Kalman filter in the case where regression coefficients follow random walks (see, e.g., Hamilton 1994). Exponential weighting is also computationally convenient because it allows recursive updating of regression coefficient estimates every period. Moreover, recursive updating also works for ridge regression. To see this, let's modify the ridge regression from (3.11) by replacing $\bar{r}_t$ with an exponentially weighted average,

$$\hat{g}_t = \left(X'X + \gamma I_K\right)^{-1} X' \left(\sum_{s=1}^{t} r_s (1-\phi)^{t-s} \phi\right), \qquad (3.28)$$

where $0 < \phi < 1$. We assume that the sample is sufficiently long so that $\sum_{s=1}^{t} (1-\phi)^{t-s} \phi \approx 1$. The estimator $\hat{g}_t$ now has a time subscript because we will consider how the estimates change when return data from additional time periods is observed. A computationally convenient property of exponential weighting is that we can express $\hat{g}_t$ as a recursively updated estimator:

$$\hat{g}_t = (1 - \phi)\hat{g}_{t-1} + \phi \left(X'X + \gamma I_K\right)^{-1} X'r_t. \tag{3.29}$$

This means that to compute the estimate for a new period, we do not need to reestimate over the whole sample. Instead, we can just use the most recent period's return data to compute the second term in (3.29) and use it to update the previous period's estimate.

Rolling windows and exponential weighting, and related techniques, are not new to asset pricing. But there are additional complications with ML techniques on high-dimensional data sets where regularization is required. In regularized methods like ridge regression and lasso, the issue is not only how to track structural change in the parameters of the prediction model, but also whether and how to adapt the values of the penalty hyperparameters over time. In the ridge regression example in (3.29) we kept the penalty parameter γ fixed, but there is not necessarily a good reason to keep it fixed over time. And if it can vary over time, we need a data-driven method to estimate how it changes over time. However, simply reestimating the penalty hyperparameters every period in overlapping rolling or expanding windows may be computationally too expensive. With big data sets, the computational burden can be substantial. To circumvent this computational burden, Monti, Anagnostopoulos, and Montana (2018) propose a recursive updating scheme for penalty hyperparameters. This is potentially a promising avenue for asset pricing applications, too.

Structural change considerations also raise questions about the suitability of CV methods for model validation and hyperparameter tuning. Typical implementations of k-fold CV presume that the temporal position of a validation fold relative to the training folds is irrelevant. Validation folds can be drawn from data that is older than some of the training data. In a stationary setting, this is fine. But when structural change is present, it is not clear that drawing validation data from time periods that precede all or part of the training data is appropriate. The direction of time can matter. A model that performs well in predicting data in backward validation folds may not necessarily perform well in predicting forward. This is an important issue for asset pricing applications of ML and there is so far little research tackling it. In Chapter 5 we will return to this question.

3.9 Concluding Remarks

In this chapter, we have explored fundamental issues that arise in the application of supervised ML techniques in asset pricing. In many ways, ML methods are well suited for prediction problems in academic research in asset pricing and in quantitative investment management. I have focused the discussion on cross-sectional asset return prediction problems, but there are other types of problems in asset pricing where supervised ML techniques could be useful. This includes, for example, applications that involve prediction of asset cash flows rather than returns, credit risk prediction, and the search for approximate hedging strategies.

The discussion in this chapter highlighted that while ML techniques can be useful, off-the-shelf application of ML methods without careful adaptation to the specific conditions of an asset pricing application is unlikely to produce good results. Prediction problems in asset pricing are in many ways substantially different from the prediction problems that most ML methods were developed for. Seemingly mundane questions such as how to scale predictor variables in data preprocessing can actually matter a lot for the performance of supervised learning algorithms. The choice between different ML methods implicitly pins down the patterns in the data—such as sparsity or the degree and type of nonlinearity—that the estimation can detect. Given the low signal-to-noise ratio in typical asset pricing settings, the idea that one could simply let the data speak and resolve these issues in a completely automatic and data-driven way without imposing substantial structure on the problem seems far-fetched.

The conclusion, therefore, is that we need an analytical framework that allows us to inject a limited amount of economic reasoning when we set up ML tools to tackle asset pricing problems. The next chapter presents an approach that makes some progress in this direction. Going beyond the simplistic example with just past returns as predictors that we examined in this chapter, we look at an application with a broader set of firm characteristics as candidate predictors. In line with the takeaways from the discussion in this chapter, the approach will take into account the important role of the covariance matrix in portfolio performance and it will allow for nonlinearities in the form of interactions between firm characteristics. Most importantly, the approach is built on a Bayesian foundation that provides a conduit to inject economic reasoning when we set up the estimation and regularization approach.

Chapter 4

ML IN CROSS-SECTIONAL ASSET PRICING

IN THE PREVIOUS CHAPTER, we outlined key issues that arise in the application of supervised learning techniques in return prediction and optimal portfolio formation. We now look at an approach that addresses many, although not all, of these issues. As in the previous chapter, the underlying analytical framework is based on Bayesian regression.

First, we look at a much broader set of covariates. In the previous chapter, the set of return predictors was limited to functions of a stock's own past returns. In this chapter, we look at an application that uses a large set of stock characteristics that have appeared as return predictors in empirical asset pricing studies. Stock return prediction analyses in this earlier pre-ML literature have looked at each of these stock characteristics in isolation, or only at small subsets of these characteristics at a time. Here we use a supervised learning approach to look at all of them jointly.

Second, building on the motivation from Section 3.5, we aggregate stock returns into portfolios weighted by these (rank-transformed and normalized) stock characteristics. These characteristics portfolios form the basis assets that span the investable universe in our analysis.

Third, facilitated by this portfolio aggregation, we incorporate the covariance matrix of these characteristics portfolio returns into the prior beliefs and the estimation approach. We leave the covariance matrix unrestricted, without imposing any special structure on it. However, we do impose structure on the relation between covariances and expected returns.

Fourth, to impose economic restrictions on the relation between covariance and expected returns, the approach in this chapter is framed in terms of a stochastic discount factor (SDF) model. Each of the characteristics portfolios is a candidate risk factor in this SDF. The parameters to be estimated are the price of risk coefficients corresponding to each of these candidate factors. These SDF weights are equivalent to portfolio weights in a mean-variance efficient portfolio. A conventional approach would be to estimate SDF coefficients with a cross-sectional regression of average returns on covariances of returns and candidate factors. Due to the large number of candidate factors, this conventional approach would

lead to spurious overfitting. Informative prior beliefs in our Bayesian setting prevent this overfitting, which helps ensure good OOS predictive
performance.

Fifth, the prior beliefs are motivated by basic asset pricing theory. Asset
pricing models of various kinds generally imply that much of the variance
of the SDF should be attributable to high-eigenvalue (i.e., high-variance)
principal components (PCs) of the candidate factor returns. Therefore,
if a factor earns high expected returns, it also should have high variance. As Kozak, Nagel, and Santosh (2018) argue, this is true not only
in rational expectations models in which pervasive macroeconomic risks
are priced, but also, under plausible restrictions, in models in which cross-
sectional variation in expected returns arises from biased investor beliefs.
The prior distribution in our approach reflects these economic considerations. Compared to the naïve ordinary least squares (OLS) estimator,
the Bayesian posterior shrinks the SDF coefficients toward zero, but the
degree of shrinkage in our case is not equal for all assets. Instead, the posterior applies significantly more shrinkage to SDF coefficients associated
with low-eigenvalue PCs.

Sixth, we also investigate whether a sparse representation of the SDF in
which only few characteristics-based factors enter the SDF is sufficient to
empirically capture the investment opportunity set. Such characteristics-
sparse SDFs are popular in the empirical asset pricing literature (see, e.g.,
Fama and French (1993) for a three factor model; Hou, Xue, and Zhang
(2015) use four factors, Fama and French (2015) use five factors, and
Barillas and Shanken (2018) suggest a six-factor model). Our baseline
Bayesian approach implies regularization with a squared L^2-norm penalty
that shrinks many SDF coefficients to nearly, but not exactly, zero. To
allow for sparsity, we augment the estimation criterion with an L^1-norm
penalty, similar to an elastic net.

Finally, we use a simple approach to allow characteristics to have
nonlinear effects. For this purpose, we augment the set of stock characteristics with second and third powers and linear first-order interactions of characteristics. The first-order interactions allow us to capture nonlinearities that empirical asset pricing studies focused on small
sets of characteristics often allow for through double-sorted portfolios.
For example, by sorting stocks into portfolios independently on two
dimensions—say, firm size and the past year's return (momentum)—
one can allow the relation between these characteristics and expected
returns and covariances to be nonlinear. The pairwise first-order interactions work in a similar way, but we form them for large numbers
of characteristics. Overall, augmenting the characteristics set with these
nonlinear transformations results in a total number of thousands of
characteristics.

The material in this chapter is an abbreviated and adapted version of Kozak, Nagel, and Santosh (2020).

4.1 Asset Pricing with Characteristics-Based Factors

We start by laying out the basic asset pricing framework that underlies characteristics-based factor models. We first describe this framework in terms of population moments, leaving aside estimation issues for now. Building on this, we can then proceed to describe the estimation problem and a supervised learning approach for dealing with the high dimensionality of this problem.

For any point in time t, let r_t denote an $N \times 1$ vector of excess returns for N stocks. Each stock has K characteristics that we collect in the $N \times K$ matrix X_t. In line with the portfolio aggregation approach outlined in the previous chapter, we use K factor portfolios formed by weighting stocks' returns with their characteristics. The factor returns are $f_t = X'_{t-1} r_t$. Then one can always find a price-of-risk vector b such that an SDF

$$M_t = 1 - b'(f_t - \mathbb{E} f_t) \qquad (4.1)$$

satisfies the unconditional pricing equation

$$\mathbb{E}[M_t f_t] = 0, \qquad (4.2)$$

where the factors f_t serve simultaneously as the assets whose returns we are trying to explain as well as the candidate factors that can potentially enter as priced factors into the SDF. The price-of-risk vector b in the SDF is at the same time also the vector of weights in the mean-variance efficient (MVE) portfolio.

In our empirical work, we cross-sectionally demean each column of X_{t-1} so that the factors in f_t are returns on zero-investment long-short portfolios. Typical characteristics-based factor models in the literature add a market factor to capture the level of the equity risk premia, while the long-short characteristics factors explain cross-sectional variation. In our specification, we focus on these cross-sectional differences. We do not explicitly include a market factor, but we orthogonalize the characteristics-based factors with respect to the market factor. This is equivalent, in terms of the effect on pricing errors, to including a market factor in the SDF. It is therefore useful here to think of the elements of f as factors that have been orthogonalized. In our empirical analysis, we also work with factors that are orthogonalized with respect to the market return.

With knowledge of population moments, we could now solve (4.1) and (4.2) for the SDF coefficients

$$b = \Sigma^{-1}\, \mathbb{E}\left(f_t\right),\tag{4.3}$$

where $\Sigma \equiv \mathbb{E}\left[\left(f_t - \mathbb{E}f_t\right)\left(f_t - \mathbb{E}f_t\right)'\right]$. Rewriting this expression as

$$b = (\Sigma\Sigma)^{-1}\,\Sigma\,\mathbb{E}\left(f_t\right)\tag{4.4}$$

shows that the SDF coefficients can be interpreted as the coefficients in a cross-sectional regression of the expected asset returns to be explained by the SDF—which, in this case, are the K elements of $\mathbb{E}[f_t]$—on the K columns of covariances of each factor with the other factors and with itself.

In practice, without knowledge of population moments, estimating the SDF coefficients by running such a cross-sectional regression in sample would result in overfitting of noise, with the consequence of poor out-of-sample performance, unless K is small. Since SDF coefficients are also weights of the MVE portfolio, the difficulty of estimating SDF coefficients with big K is closely related to the well-known problem of estimating the weights of the MVE portfolio when the number of assets is large. The supervised learning approach we use is designed to address this problem.

Much of the existing characteristics-based factor model literature has sidestepped this high-dimensionality problem by focusing on models that include only a small number of factors. We will refer to such models as characteristics-sparse models. Whether such a characteristics-sparse model can adequately describe the SDF in a cross-section with a large number of stock characteristics is a key empirical question that the empirical results reported in this chapter shed light on.

Kozak, Nagel, and Santosh (2020) point out that there are no strong economic reasons to expect characteristics-sparsity of the SDF. However, one may be able to find rotations of the characteristics factor data that admit, at least approximately, a sparse SDF representation. Kozak, Nagel, and Santosh (2018) argue that absence of near-arbitrage (extremely high Sharpe ratios) implies that factors earning substantial risk premia must be major sources of co-movement. This conclusion obtains under very mild assumptions and applies equally to "rational" and "behavioral" models. Furthermore, for typical sets of test assets, returns have a strong factor structure dominated by a small number of PCs with the highest variance. Under these two conditions, an SDF with a small number of these high-variance PCs as factors should explain most of the cross-sectional variation in expected returns. Motivated by this theoretical result, we explore empirically whether an SDF sparse in PCs can be sufficient to describe the cross-section of expected returns, and we compare it, in terms of pricing performance, with SDFs that are sparse in characteristics.

To construct the PC factors, we use the eigendecomposition of the factor covariance matrix,

$$\Sigma = Q\Lambda Q' \quad \text{with} \quad \Lambda = \text{diag}(\lambda_1, \lambda_2, \ldots, \lambda_H), \tag{4.5}$$

where Q is the matrix of eigenvectors of Σ, and Λ is the diagonal matrix of eigenvalues ordered in decreasing magnitude. Using the eigenvectors as portfolio weights, we obtain the PC factors

$$p_t = Q'f_t. \tag{4.6}$$

Using all PCs, and with knowledge of population moments, we could express the SDF as

$$M_t = 1 - b_P' (p_t - \mathbb{E}p_t), \quad \text{with} \quad b_P = \Lambda^{-1} \mathbb{E}[p_t]. \tag{4.7}$$

4.2   Supervised Learning Approach

We now describe the supervised learning approach to estimate the SDF parameter vector b (or b_P in the case where we use the PC factors). The method is a variant of the Bayesian regression that we discussed in Chapters 2 and 3.

Consider a sample with size T. We denote

$$\bar{\mu} = \frac{1}{T} \sum_{t=1}^{T} f_t, \tag{4.8}$$

$$\bar{\Sigma} = \frac{1}{T} \sum_{t=1}^{T} (f_t - \bar{\mu}) (f_t - \bar{\mu})'. \tag{4.9}$$

A natural, but naïve, estimator of the coefficients b of the SDF in (4.1) could be constructed based on the sample moment conditions

$$\bar{\mu} - \frac{1}{T} \sum_{t=1}^{T} f_t = 0, \tag{4.10}$$

$$\frac{1}{T} \sum_{t=1}^{T} M_t(\hat{b}, \bar{\mu}) f_t = 0. \tag{4.11}$$

Solving for $\hat{b}$, the resulting estimator is the sample version of (4.3):

$$\hat{b} = \bar{\Sigma}^{-1} \bar{\mu}. \tag{4.12}$$

However, unless K is very small relative to T, this naïve estimator yields very imprecise estimates of b. The main source of imprecision is the uncertainty about μ. Note that one can rewrite the naïve estimator as an OLS regression estimator $\hat{b} = (\overline{\Sigma}\,\overline{\Sigma})^{-1}\overline{\Sigma}\bar{\mu}$, i.e., a cross-sectional regression of factor means on the covariances of these factors with each other. As is generally the case in expected return estimation, the factor mean estimates are imprecise even with fairly long samples of returns. In a high-dimensional setting with large K, the cross-sectional regression effectively has a large number of explanatory variables. As a consequence, the regression will end up spuriously overfitting the huge noise component in the factor means, resulting in a very imprecise $\hat{b}$ estimate and bad out-of-sample performance. Estimation uncertainty in the covariance matrix can further exacerbate the problem, but as discussed in more detail in Kozak, Nagel, and Santosh (2020), the main source of fragility in this setting are the factor means, not the covariances.

To avoid spurious overfitting, we bring in economically motivated prior beliefs about the factors' expected returns. If the prior beliefs are well motivated and truly informative, this will help reduce the (posterior) uncertainty about the SDF coefficients. In other words, bringing in prior information regularizes the estimation problem sufficiently to produce robust estimates that perform well in out-of-sample prediction. We first start with prior beliefs that shrink the SDF coefficients away from the naïve estimator in (4.12) but without imposing sparsity. We then expand the framework to allow for some degree of sparsity as well.

4.2.1 Shrinkage Estimator

To focus on uncertainty about factor means, the most important source of fragility in the estimation, we proceed under the assumption that Σ is known. We impose the following prior beliefs about expected returns of the K factor portfolios

$$\mu \sim \mathcal{N}\left(0, \frac{\kappa^2}{\tau}\Sigma^2\right), \tag{4.13}$$

where $\tau = \text{tr}\,[\Sigma]$, and κ is a constant controlling the "scale" of μ that may depend on τ and K.

To understand the economic implications of these prior beliefs, it is useful to consider the PC portfolios $p_t = Q'f_t$ with $\Sigma = Q\Lambda Q'$ that we introduced in Section 4.1. Expressing the prior (4.13) in terms of PC portfolios, we get

$$\mu_P \sim \mathcal{N}\left(0, \frac{\kappa^2}{\tau}\mathbf{\Lambda}^2\right). \tag{4.14}$$

For the prior distribution of Sharpe ratios of the PCs, we obtain

$$\mathbf{\Lambda}^{-\frac{1}{2}}\mu_P \sim \mathcal{N}\left(0, \frac{\kappa^2}{\tau}\mathbf{\Lambda}\right). \tag{4.15}$$

Hence, this prior belief specification implies that big magnitudes of Sharpe ratios are more likely to arise for PCs with high eigenvalues, i.e., for portfolios that load on major sources of return covariances. In contrast, for PCs with low eigenvalues, i.e., portfolios that load mostly on more idiosyncratic types of risk, Sharpe ratios are likely to be close to zero.

These prior beliefs are broadly in line with a wide variety of asset pricing models. For instance, in rational expectations models in which cross-sectional differences in expected returns arise from exposure to macroeconomic risk factors, risk premia are typically concentrated in one or a few common factors. This means that Sharpe ratios of low-eigenvalue PCs should be smaller than those of the high-eigenvalue PCs that are the major source of risk premia. Kozak, Nagel, and Santosh (2018) show that a similar prediction also arises in plausible behavioral models in which investors have biased beliefs. They argue that to be economically plausible, such a model should include arbitrageurs in the investor population, and it should have realistic position size limits (e.g., leverage constraints or limits on short selling) for the biased-belief investors (who are likely to be less sophisticated). As a consequence, biased beliefs can only have substantial pricing effects in the cross-section if the variation in these biased beliefs across stocks aligns with high-eigenvalue PCs; otherwise, arbitrageurs would find it too attractive to aggressively lean against the demand from biased investors, leaving very little price impact. To the extent it exists, mispricing then appears in the SDF mainly through the risk prices of high-eigenvalue PCs. Thus, within both classes of asset pricing models, we would expect high magnitudes of Sharpe ratios to be more likely for high-eigenvalue PCs, which is consistent with the prior beliefs we specified here.

Another way to think about these priors is to imagine an investor who is analyzing the historical data with the goal of forming a mean-variance optimized portfolio. In a market that has at least some active arbitrageurs preventing extreme forms of mispricing, the investor should expect, a priori, that the optimal portfolio does not involve extremely large positive or negative portfolio weights. Since the optimal portfolio weights of a rational investor and SDF coefficients are equivalent, this means that the sum of squared SDF coefficients, $b'b$, should remain bounded below some value that is not extremely high. A minimal requirement for this to be true is that $\mathbb{E}[b'b]$ remains bounded (for a given K). Under the prior (4.13) we have

$$\mathbb{E}[b'b] = \frac{\kappa^2}{\tau}K, \tag{4.16}$$

which does not depend on Λ and can be kept at moderate levels with an appropriate choice of κ. As Kozak, Nagel, and Santosh (2020) discuss, if the exponent of Σ in (4.13) was some $\eta < 2$ instead of $\eta = 2$, then the SDF coefficients associated with some low-eigenvalue PCs could take extremely high values, leading to very high $\mathbb{E}[b'b]$ and implying the optimal portfolio of a rational investor would place huge bets on the lowest-eigenvalue PCs—which seems implausible.

Based on the assumption (4.13), we get an independent and identically distributed (i.i.d.) prior on SDF coefficients, $b \sim \mathcal{N}\left(0, \frac{\kappa^2}{\tau}I_K\right)$. Combining these prior beliefs with information about sample means $\bar{\mu}$ from a sample with size T, assuming a multivariate-normal likelihood, we obtain the posterior mean of b

$$\hat{b} = (\Sigma + \gamma I_K)^{-1}\bar{\mu}, \tag{4.17}$$

where $\gamma = \frac{\tau}{\kappa^2 T}$. To map this estimator back to the Bayesian regression (2.22) that we discussed in Section 2.4, note that one can rewrite the naïve estimator in (4.12), now with known Σ, as a GLS regression estimator: $\left(\Sigma\Sigma^{-1}\Sigma\right)^{-1}\Sigma\Sigma^{-1}\bar{\mu}$. Imposing an informative prior with covariance matrix $\Sigma_g = \frac{\kappa^2}{\tau}I_K$, the estimator then maps exactly into the Bayesian regression posterior mean in (2.22) and (4.17).

Setting this up as a Bayesian estimation problem avoids the rescaling problem we discussed in the previous chapter. For example, if we transformed the factors f_t with a nonsingular matrix Hf_t, one can show that the posterior mean that corresponds to (4.17) for the SDF coefficients for these transformed factors is $\hat{b}_H = (H')^{-1}\hat{b}$. As a consequence, the resulting estimated SDF $M_t = 1 - \hat{b}'H^{-1}(Hf_t - \mathbb{E}Hf_t) = 1 - \hat{b}'(f_t - \mathbb{E}f_t)$ remains invariant to this transformation of the factors.

ECONOMIC INTERPRETATION

To provide an economic interpretation of what this estimator does, it is convenient to consider a rotation of the original space of returns into the space of principal components. Expressing the SDF based on the estimator (4.17) in terms of PC portfolio returns, $p_t = Q'f_t$, with coefficients $\hat{b}_P =$

$Q'\hat{b}$, we obtain a price-of-risk vector with elements

$$\hat{b}_{P,j} = \left(\frac{\lambda_j}{\lambda_j + \gamma} \right) \frac{\bar{\mu}_{P,j}}{\lambda_j}. \tag{4.18}$$

Compared with the naïve exactly identified GMM estimator from (4.12), which would yield SDF coefficients for the PCs of

$$\hat{b}_{P,j}^{\text{ols}} = \frac{\bar{\mu}_{P,j}}{\lambda_j}, \tag{4.19}$$

our Bayesian estimator (with $\gamma > 0$) shrinks the SDF coefficients toward zero with the shrinkage factor $\lambda_j/(\lambda_j + \gamma) < 1$. Most importantly, the shrinkage is stronger the smaller the eigenvalue λ_j associated with the PC. The economic interpretation is that under the prior beliefs we specified, we judge as implausible that a PC with low eigenvalue could contribute substantially to the volatility of the SDF and hence to the overall maximum squared Sharpe ratio. For this reason, the estimator shrinks the SDF coefficients of these low-eigenvalue PCs particularly strongly.

REPRESENTATION AS A PENALIZED ESTIMATOR

As we discussed in Section 2.4, the Bayesian estimator maps into a penalized regression estimator. If we maximize the model cross-sectional R^2 for explaining mean returns subject to a penalty on the model-implied maximum squared Sharpe ratio $\gamma b' \Sigma b$,

$$\hat{b} = \arg\min_b \left\{ (\bar{\mu} - \Sigma b)' (\bar{\mu} - \Sigma b) + \gamma b' \Sigma b \right\}, \tag{4.20}$$

the problem leads to exactly the same solution as in (4.17). The objective in (4.20) resembles a ridge regression objective, but with some important differences. A standard ridge regression objective function would impose a penalty on the squared L^2-norm of coefficients, $b'b$, while the objective in (4.20) penalizes $\gamma b' \Sigma b$.

We can also rewrite the criterion in (4.20) equivalently as

$$\hat{b} = \arg\min_b \left\{ (\bar{\mu} - \Sigma b)' \Sigma^{-1} (\bar{\mu} - \Sigma b) + \gamma b'b \right\}. \tag{4.21}$$

In this formulation, the estimator penalizes $b'b$ as in a standard ridge regression, but the loss function is different because errors are weighted by Σ^{-1}, akin to a GLS regression. This way of writing the estimation criterion is useful for introducing a sparsity-inducing penalty.

4.2.2 Sparsity

The method that we have presented so far deals with the high-dimensionality challenge by shrinking SDF coefficients toward zero, but none of the coefficients are set to exactly zero. In other words, the solution we obtain is not sparse. As we have argued in Section 4.1, the economic case for extreme sparsity with characteristics-based factors is weak. However, it may be useful to allow for the possibility that some factors are truly redundant in terms of their contribution to the SDF. Moreover, as we have discussed, there are economic reasons to expect that a representation of the SDF that is sparse in terms of PCs could provide a good approximation. Sparsity could therefore be useful when we consider PCs as factors.

For these reasons, we now introduce an additional L^1 penalty $\gamma_1 \sum_{j=1}^{H} |b_j|$ in the penalized regression problem given by (4.21). The approach is motivated by lasso regression and elastic net and it leads to some elements of $\hat{b}$ being set to zero. Combining both L^1 and L^2 penalties, our estimator solves the problem:[1]

$$\hat{b} = \arg\min_{b} \left(\bar{\mu} - \Sigma b\right)' \Sigma^{-1} \left(\bar{\mu} - \Sigma b\right) + \gamma_2 b'b + \gamma_1 \sum_{j=1}^{H} |b_j|. \qquad (4.22)$$

This dual-penalty method enjoys much of the economic motivation behind the L^2-penalty-only method with an added benefit of potentially delivering sparse SDF representations. We can control the degree of sparsity by varying the strength of the L^1 penalty and the degree of economic shrinkage by varying the L^2 penalty.

While we will ultimately let the data speak about the optimal values of the penalties γ_1 and γ_2, there is reason to believe that completely switching off the L^2 penalty and focusing purely on lasso-style estimation would not work well in this asset pricing setting. Lasso is known to suffer from relatively poor performance compared with ridge and elastic net when regressors are correlated (Tibshirani 1996, Zou and Hastie 2005). As we discussed in Section 2.2.1, the tendency of L^1-penalized estimation to pick one of two correlated variables, rather than averaging them, hurts predictive performance if correlated covariates each contain a common signal and uncorrelated noise. For instance, rather than picking book-to-market as the only characteristic to represent the value effect in an SDF, it may be advantageous to consider a weighted average of multiple measures of value, such as book-to-market, price-dividend, and cash flow-to-price

---

[1]To solve the optimization problem in (4.22), we use the LARS-EN algorithm in Zou and Hastie (2005).

ratios. This reasoning also suggests that an L^1-only penalty may work better when we first transform the characteristics-based factors into their PCs before estimation. We examine this question in our empirical work below.

4.2.3   Data-Driven Penalty Choice

To implement the estimators (4.17) and (4.22), we need to set the values of the penalty parameters γ, γ_1, and γ_2. In the L^2-only penalty specification, the penalty parameter $\gamma = \frac{\tau}{\kappa^2 T}$ following from the prior (4.13) has an economic interpretation. The root expected maximum squared Sharpe ratio under the prior is

$$\mathbb{E}[\boldsymbol{\mu}'\boldsymbol{\Sigma}^{-1}\boldsymbol{\mu}]^{1/2} = \kappa. \tag{4.23}$$

This means that $\gamma = \frac{\tau}{\kappa^2 T}$ implicitly represents views about the maximum squared Sharpe ratio. For example, an expectation that the maximum Sharpe ratio cannot be very high, i.e., low κ, would imply high γ and hence a high degree of shrinkage imposed on the estimation. Some researchers pick a prior belief based on intuitive reasoning about the likely relationship between the maximum squared Sharpe ratio and the historical squared Sharpe ratio of a market index.[2] However, these are intuitive guesses. It would be difficult to go further and ground beliefs about κ in deeper economic analyses of plausible degrees of risk aversion, risk-bearing capacity of arbitrageurs, and degree of mispricing. For this reason, we prefer a data-driven approach. But we will make use of (4.23) to express the magnitude of the L^2-penalty that we apply in estimation in terms of an economically interpretable root expected maximum squared Sharpe ratio.

We use a data-driven approach that involves estimation of γ via k-fold cross-validation (CV). We divide the historic data into k equal subsamples. Then, for each possible γ (or each possible pair of γ_1, γ_2 in the dual-penalty specification), we compute $\hat{b}$ by applying (4.17) to $k-1$ of these subsamples. We evaluate the OOS fit of the resulting model on the single withheld subsample. Consistent with the penalized objective, (4.20), we compute the OOS R-squared as

$$R_{\text{oos}}^2 = 1 - \frac{\left(\bar{\boldsymbol{\mu}}_2 - \overline{\boldsymbol{\Sigma}}_2\hat{b}\right)'\left(\bar{\boldsymbol{\mu}}_2 - \overline{\boldsymbol{\Sigma}}_2\hat{b}\right)}{\bar{\boldsymbol{\mu}}_2'\bar{\boldsymbol{\mu}}_2}, \tag{4.24}$$

---

[2] Barillas and Shanken (2018) is a recent example. See also MacKinlay (1995) and Ross (1976) for similar arguments.

where the subscript 2 indicates an OOS sample moment from the with-held sample. We repeat this procedure k times, each time treating a different subsample as the OOS data. We then average the R^2 across these k estimates, yielding the cross-validated R^2_{oos}. Finally, we choose γ (or γ_1, γ_2) that generates the highest R^2_{oos}.

We chose $k = 3$ as a compromise between estimation uncertainty in $\hat{b}$ and estimation uncertainty in the OOS covariance matrix $\overline{\Sigma}_2$. The latter type of uncertainty increases with k. With high k, the withheld sample becomes too short for $\overline{\Sigma}_2$ to be well behaved, which distorts the fit-ted factor mean returns $\overline{\Sigma}_2\hat{b}$. However, our results are robust to using moderately higher k.

This penalty choice procedure uses information from the whole sample to find the penalty parameters that minimize the R^2 based on Eq. (30). The cross-validated OOS R^2 at the optimal values of the penalty param-eters is therefore typically an upward-biased estimate of the true OOS R^2 that one would obtain in a new data set that has not been used for penalty parameter estimation (Varma and Simon (2006), Tibshirani and Tibshi-rani (2009)). Our interest centers on the optimal strength of regularization and we therefore are only concerned about the relative performance of models at various degrees of regularization, not the level of the OOS R^2. In a subsequent step, in Section 4.4, we also evaluate the penalty param-eter choice OOS by applying the estimated SDF on a part of the sample that has not been used to estimate the penalty parameters.

4.3 Empirical Analysis

We start with the universe of US firms in the CRSP database. We construct two independent sets of characteristics. The first set relies on characteris-tics underlying common "anomalies" in the literature. We follow standard anomaly definitions in Novy-Marx and Velikov (2016), McLean and Pon-tiff (2016), Kogan and Tian (2015), and Hou, Xue, and Zhang (2015) and compile our own set of 50 such characteristics. The second set of characteristics is based on 70 financial ratios as defined by Wharton Research Data Services (WRDS): the WRDS Industry Financial Ratios (WFR), a collection of over 70 financial ratios grouped into the following seven categories: capitalization, efficiency, financial soundness/solvency, liquidity, profitability, valuation, and others. We supplement this data set with 12 portfolios sorted on past monthly returns in months $t - 1$ through $t - 12$. The combined data set contains 80 managed portfolios (we drop two variables due to their short time series and end up with 68 WRDS ratios in the final data set). The Internet Appendix of Kozak,

Nagel, and Santosh (2020) provides definitions of all variables in both data sets.

To focus exclusively on the cross-sectional aspect of return predictability, remove the influence of outliers, and keep constant leverage across all portfolios, we perform certain normalizations of characteristics that define our characteristics-based factors. First, we perform a simple rank transformation for each characteristic. For each characteristic i of a stock s at a given time t, denoted as $c_{s,t}^i$, we sort all stocks based on the values of their respective characteristics $c_{s,t}^i$ and rank them cross-sectionally (across all s) from 1 to n_t, where n_t is the number of stocks at t for which this characteristic is available.[3] We then normalize all ranks by dividing by $n_t + 1$ to obtain the value of the rank transform

$$rc_{s,t}^i = \frac{\text{rank}\left(c_{s,t}^i\right)}{n_t + 1}. \tag{4.25}$$

Next, we normalize each rank-transformed characteristic $rc_{s,t}^i$ by first centering it cross-sectionally and then dividing by sum of absolute deviations from the mean of all stocks

$$x_{s,t}^i = \frac{\left(rc_{s,t}^i - \bar{rc}_t^i\right)}{\sum_{s=1}^{n_t} \left|rc_{s,t}^i - \bar{rc}_t^i\right|}, \tag{4.26}$$

where $\bar{rc}_t^i = \frac{1}{n_t} \sum_{s=1}^{n_t} rc_{s,t}^i$. The resulting zero-investment long-short portfolios of transformed characteristics $x_{s,t}^i$ are insensitive to outliers and allow us to keep the absolute amount of long and short positions invested in the characteristic-based strategy (i.e., leverage) fixed. For instance, doubling the number of stocks at any time t has no effect on the strategy's gross exposure.[4] Finally, we combine all transformed characteristics $x_{s,t}^i$ for all stocks into a matrix of instruments X_t.[5] Interaction with returns, $f_t = X_{t-1}' r_t$, then yields one factor for each characteristic.

To ensure that the results are not driven by very small illiquid stocks, we exclude small-cap stocks with market caps below 0.01% of aggregate stock market capitalization at the time of portfolio formation.[6] In all of our analysis, we use daily returns from CRSP for each individual stock.

---

[3]If two stocks are "tied," we assign the average rank to both. For example, if two firms have the lowest value of c, they are both assigned a rank of 1.5 (the average of 1 and 2). This preserves any symmetry in the underlying characteristic.

[4]Since the portfolio is long-short, the net exposure is always zero.

[5]If $x_{s,t}^i$ is missing we replace it with the mean value, zero.

[6]For example, for an aggregate stock market capitalization of $20 trillion, we keep only stocks with market caps above $2 billion.

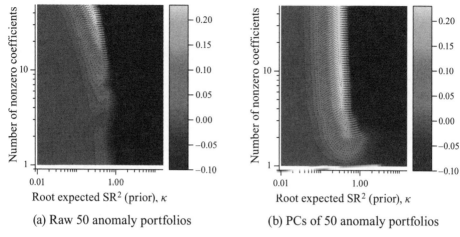

(a) Raw 50 anomaly portfolios   (b) PCs of 50 anomaly portfolios

Figure 4.1. OOS R^2 from dual-penalty specification (50 anomaly portfolios). OOS cross-sectional R^2 for families of models that employ both L^1 and L^2 penalties simultaneously using 50 anomaly portfolios (Panel a) and 50 PCs based on anomaly portfolios (Panel b). We quantify the strength of the L^2 penalty by prior root expected squared Sharpe ratio on the x-axis. We show the number of retained variables in the SDF, which quantifies the strength of the L^1 penalty, on the y-axis. Both axes are plotted on logarithmic scale.

Using daily data allows us to estimate second moments much more precisely than with monthly data and focus on uncertainty in means while largely ignoring uncertainty in covariance estimates (with exceptions as noted below). We adjust daily portfolio weights on individual stocks within each month to correspond to a monthly rebalanced buy-and-hold strategy during that month. Finally, we orthogonalize all portfolio returns with respect to the CRSP value-weighted index return using market factor loadings estimated in the full sample.

4.3.1   Fifty Anomaly Characteristics

We start with the data set of 50 portfolios based on anomaly characteristics. The sample is daily from November 1973 to December 2017. Figure 4.1 presents the OOS R^2 from our dual-penalty specification as a function of κ (on the x-axis) and the number of nonzero SDF coefficients (on the y-axis). Focusing on the left-hand part of Figure 4.1 based on raw returns of the 50 anomaly portfolios, unregularized models (top-right corner) demonstrate extremely poor performance with OOS R^2 substantially below zero. Hence, substantial regularization is needed to get good OOS performance. Moreover, there is not much substitutability between

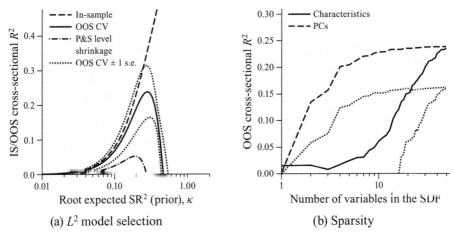

(a) L^2 model selection   (b) Sparsity

Figure 4.2. L^2 **model selection and sparsity (50 anomaly portfolios).** Panel (a) plots the in-sample cross-sectional R^2 (dashed), OOS cross-sectional R^2 based on cross-validation (solid), and OOS cross-sectional R^2 based on the proportional shrinkage (dash-dot) from Pástor and Stambaugh (2000). In Panel (b), we show the maximum OOS cross-sectional R^2 attained by a model with n factors (on the x-axis) across all possible values of L^2 shrinkage, for models based on original characteristics portfolios (solid) and PCs (dashed). Dotted lines in Panel (b) depict -1 s.e. bounds of the CV estimator.

L^1- and L^2-regularization. To attain the maximum OOS R^2, the data calls for substantial L^2-shrinkage but essentially no sparsity. Imposing sparsity (i.e., moving down in the plot) leads to a major deterioration in OOS R^2. This indicates that there is almost no redundancy among the 50 anomalies. To adequately capture the pricing information in the 50 anomalies, one needs to include basically all of these 50 factors in the SDF. Shrinking their SDF coefficients is important for obtaining good performance, but forcing any of them to zero to get a sparse solution hurts the OOS R^2. In other words, a characteristics-sparse SDF with good pricing performance does not exist. Hence, many anomaly portfolio factors make substantial marginal contributions to the OOS explanatory power of the SDF.

If we take the PCs of the anomaly portfolio returns as basis assets, as shown in right-hand part of Figure 4.1, the situation is quite different. A relatively sparse SDF with only four PCs, for example, does quite well in terms of OOS R^2, and with ten PCs we get close to the maximum OOS R^2. Thus, a PC-sparse SDF prices the anomaly portfolios quite well.

Figure 4.2 provides a more precise picture of the key properties of OOS R^2 by taking cuts of the contour plots. The solid line in the left-hand side plot represents a cut along the top edge of Figure 4.1 with varying degrees of L^2-shrinkage but no sparsity. As the figure shows, the OOS R^2 is maximized for $\kappa \approx 0.30$. The standard error bounds indicate that OOS R^2 around this value of κ is not only economically but also statistically quite far above zero.

In Section 4.2.1, we argued on economic grounds that our prior (4.13) with variance proportional to Σ^2 is reasonable. However, it would be useful to check whether this economic motivation is also accompanied by better performance in the data. To do this, the dash-dot line in the left-hand side figure plots the OOS R^2 we would get with the more commonly used prior of Pástor and Stambaugh (2000), where the prior variance is proportional to Σ rather than Σ^2. Recall that our method performs both level shrinkage of all coefficients, as well as relative shrinkage (twist) that downweights the influence of low-eigenvalue PCs. The method in Pástor and Stambaugh (2000) employs only level shrinkage. We can see that optimally chosen level shrinkage alone achieves OOS R^2 lower than 5% (an improvement over the OLS solution) but falls substantially short of the 30% R^2 delivered by our method.[7] Relative shrinkage, which is the key element of our method, therefore contributes a major fraction of the total out-of-sample performance.

The right-hand side graph in Figure 4.2 takes a cut in the contour plots along the ridge of maximal OOS R^2 from bottom to top, where we vary sparsity and choose the optimal L^2-shrinkage for each level of sparsity. The solid line shows very clearly how characteristics-sparse SDFs perform poorly. The OOS R^2 only starts rising substantially at the lowest sparsity levels toward the very right of the plot. In PC space, on the contrary, very sparse models perform exceedingly well: a model with only two PC-based factors captures roughly two-thirds of the total OOS cross-sectional R^2. A model with ten PC factors achieves nearly maximal R^2, while a model with ten factors in the space of characteristics-based factors achieves less than a third of the maximum.

To summarize, there is little redundancy among the 50 anomalies. As a consequence, it is not possible to find a sparse SDF with just a few characteristics-based factors that delivers good OOS performance. For this reason, it is also important to deal with the high-dimensional nature of the estimation problem through an L^2-shrinkage rather than just an L^1-penalty and sparsity. L^2-shrinkage delivers much higher OOS R^2 than a pure L^1-penalty lasso-style approach, and the dual-penalty approach with data-driven penalty choice essentially turns off the L^1 penalty for

---

[7] For the Pástor and Stambaugh (2000) level shrinkage estimator, we show the expected maximum squared Sharpe ratio under the prior on the x-axis, but it no longer coincides with the κ parameter in this case.

this set of portfolios. However, if these portfolio returns are transformed into their PCs, a sparse representation of the SDF emerges. These findings are consistent with the point we made in Section 4.1 that the economic arguments for a characteristics-sparse SDF are rather weak, while there are good reasons to expect approximate sparsity in terms of PCs.

4.3.2   WRDS Financial Ratios (WFR)

The data set of 50 anomalies is special in the sense that all of these characteristics are known, from the past literature, to be related to average returns. Our method is useful for checking for redundancy among these anomalies, but this set of asset returns did not expose the method to the challenge of identifying entirely new pricing factors from a high-dimensional data set. For this reason, we now look at 80 factors formed based on the WFR data set. The sample is daily from September 1964 to December 2017. Some of the characteristics in the WFR data set are known to be related to expected returns (e.g., several versions of the P/E ratio), but many others are not. It is therefore possible that a substantial number of these 80 factors are irrelevant for pricing. It will be interesting to see whether our method can properly de-emphasize these pricing-irrelevant factors and avoid overfitting them.

The contour map of OOS R^2 in Figure 4.3 looks quite similar to the earlier one for the 50 anomaly portfolios in Figure 4.1. Unregularized models (top-right corner) again perform extremely poorly with OOS R^2 significantly below zero. L^2-penalty-only based models (top edge of a plot) perform well for both raw portfolio returns and PCs. L^1-penalty-only "lasso" based models (right edge of the plot) work poorly for raw portfolio returns in the left-hand figure.

However, there are some differences as well. As can be seen toward the right edge of the right-hand side figure, a PC-sparse SDF not only does quite well in terms of OOS R^2, but it does so even without much L^2-shrinkage. A potential explanation of this finding is that the data mining and publication bias toward in-sample significant factors may play a bigger role in the anomalies data set, which is based on published anomalies, than in the WFR data set. As a consequence, stronger shrinkage of SDF coefficients toward zero may be needed in the anomalies data set to prevent these biases from impairing OOS performance, while there is less need for shrinkage in the WFR data set because in- and out-of-sample returns are not so different.

This explanation is further consistent with the fact that the OOS R^2-maximizing $\kappa \approx 1$, which is much higher than in the anomalies data set. The left-hand side plot in Figure 4.4 illustrates this even more

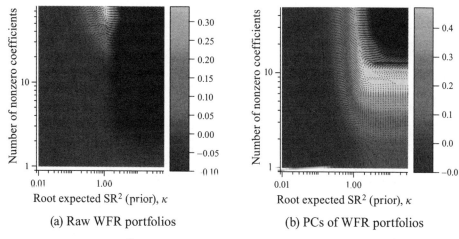

(a) Raw WFR portfolios   (b) PCs of WFR portfolios

Figure 4.3. **OOS R^2 from dual-penalty specification (WFR portfolios).** OOS cross-sectional R^2 for families of models that employ both L^1 and L^2 penalties simultaneously using 80 WFR portfolios (Panel a) and 80 PCs based on WFR portfolios (Panel b). We quantify the strength of the L^2 penalty by prior root expected squared Sharpe ratio on the x-axis. We show the number of retained variables in the SDF, which quantifies the strength of the L^1 penalty, on the y-axis. Both axes are plotted on logarithmic scale.

transparently by taking a cut along the top edge of the left-hand side contour plot in Figure 4.3. The solid line shows the OOS R^2. Its peak is much farther to the right than in the analogous figure for the anomalies data set (Figure 4.2), consistent with our intuition that WFR are less likely to have been datamined in an early part of the sample compared to the published anomalies and therefore do not require as much shrinkage. Standard errors are smaller, too, due to more stable performance of WFR portfolios across time periods relative to anomalies, which experienced significant deterioration in the latest (not datamined) part of the sample (McLean and Pontiff 2016).

The right-hand side graph in Figure 4.4 takes a cut in the contour plots along the ridge of maximal OOS R^2 from bottom to top where we vary sparsity and choose the optimal shrinkage for each level of sparsity. This figure illustrates that as in the case of the 50 anomalies, there is little sparsity in the space of characteristics. Even so, sparsity is again much stronger in PC space. A model with six factors delivers nearly maximum OOS R^2.

In summary, the analysis of the WFR data set shows that our method can handle well a data set that mixes factors that are relevant for pricing with others that are not. If sparsity is desired, a moderate level of

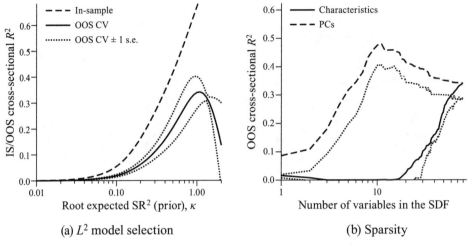

(a) L^2 model selection   (b) Sparsity

Figure 4.4. L^2 **model selection and sparsity (WFR portfolios).** Panel (a) plots the in-sample cross-sectional R^2 (dashed) and OOS cross-sectional R^2 based on cross-validation (solid). In Panel (b), we show the maximum OOS cross-sectional R^2 attained by a model with n factors (on the x-axis) across all possible values of L^2 shrinkage for models based on original characteristics portfolios (solid) and PCs (dashed). Dotted lines in Panel (b) depict -1 s.e. bounds of the CV estimator.

L^1-penalty can be used to omit the pricing-irrelevant factors, but a L^2-penalty-only method works just as well in terms of OOS R^2.

4.3.3   Interactions

To raise the statistical challenge, we now consider extremely high-dimensional data sets. We supplement the sets of 50 anomaly and 80 WFR raw characteristics with additional ones constructed as second and third powers and linear first-order interactions of the raw characteristics. This exercise is interesting not only in terms of the statistical challenge but also because it allows us to relax the rather arbitrary assumption that characteristics-based factor portfolio weights are linear in (ranked and normalized) characteristics.

In fact, for some anomalies like the idiosyncratic volatility anomaly, it is known that the expected return effect is concentrated among stocks with extreme values of the characteristic. Fama and French (2008) and Freyberger, Neuhierl, and Weber (2020) provide evidence of nonlinear effects for other anomalies but in terms of portfolio sorts and cross-sectional return prediction rather than SDF estimation. Furthermore, while there is existing evidence of interaction effects for a few anomalies (Asness, Moskowitz, and Pedersen 2013, Fama and French 2008), interactions have not been explored in the pre-ML empirical asset pricing literature for more than these few—presumably a consequence of the extreme high dimensionality of the problem. Interactions expand the set of possible predictors exponentially. For instance, with only first-order interactions of 50 raw characteristics and their powers, we obtain $\frac{1}{2}n(n+1)+2n=1{,}375$ candidate factors and test asset returns. For 80 WFR characteristics, we obtain a set of 3,400 portfolios.

We construct the nonlinear weights and interactions as follows. For any two given rank-transformed characteristics $x^i_{s,t}$ and $x^j_{s,t}$ of a stock s at time t, we define the first-order interaction characteristic $x^{ij}_{s,t}$ as the product of two original characteristics that is further renormalized using (4.26) as follows:

$$x^{ij}_{s,t} = \frac{\left(x^i_{s,t}x^j_{s,t} - \frac{1}{n_t}\sum_{s=1}^{n_t} x^i_{s,t}x^j_{s,t}\right)}{\sum_{s=1}^{n_t}\left|x^i_{s,t}x^j_{s,t} - \frac{1}{n_t}\sum_{s=1}^{n_t} x^i_{s,t}x^j_{s,t}\right|}. \tag{4.27}$$

We include all first-order interactions in our empirical tests. In addition to interactions, we also include second and third powers of each characteristic, which are defined analogously based on interaction of the characteristic with itself. Note that although we renormalize all characteristics after interacting or raising to powers, we do not rerank them. For example, the cube of any given characteristic then is a new different characteristic that has stronger exposures to stocks with extreme realization of the original characteristic but has the same gross exposure (leverage). The Internet Appendix of Kozak, Nagel, and Santosh (2020) illustrates how this approach maps into more conventional two-way portfolio sorts.

Due to the extremely high number of characteristics-based factors in this case, our three-fold cross-validation method runs into numerical instability issues in covariance matrix inversion, even with daily data. For this reason, we switch to two-fold cross-validation. This gives us a somewhat longer sample to estimate the covariance matrix, and this sample extension is sufficient to obtain stable behavior.[8]

Figure 4.5 shows contour maps of the OOS cross-sectional R^2 as a function of κ (on the x-axis) and the number of nonzero SDF coefficients (on the y-axis). Plots for the raw portfolio returns are shown in the top row, and plots for the PCs are in the bottom row. Focusing first on the

---

[8] Because some interactions are missing in the earlier part of the sample, our sample periods shorten to February 1974–December 2017 and September 1968–December 2017 for anomaly and WFR characteristics, respectively.

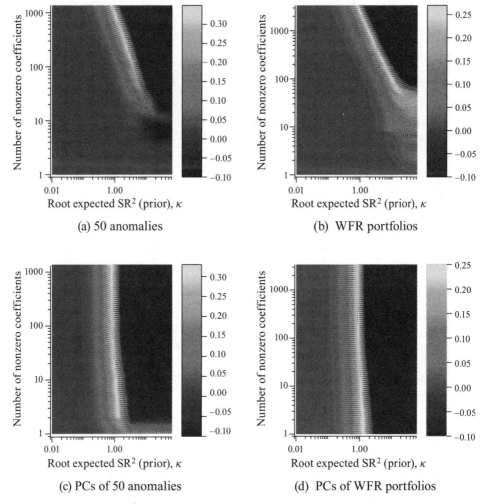

Figure 4.5. **OOS R^2 from dual-penalty specification for models with interactions.** OOS cross-sectional R^2 for families of models that employ both L^1 and L^2 penalties simultaneously using portfolio returns based on interactions of 50 anomaly (Panel a) and 80 WFR (Panel b) characteristics and PCs of these portfolio returns (Panels c and d). We quantify the strength of the L^2 penalty by prior root expected squared Sharpe ratio on the x-axis. We show the number of retained variables in the SDF, which quantifies the strength of the L^1 penalty, on the y-axis. Both axes are plotted on logarithmic scale.

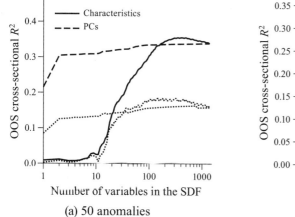
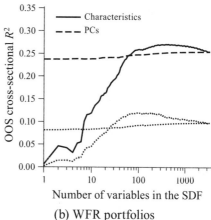

(a) 50 anomalies

(b) WFR portfolios

Figure 4.6. L^1 **sparsity of models with interactions.** We show the maximum OOS cross-sectional R^2 attained by a model with n factors (on the x-axis) across all possible values of L^2 shrinkage for models based on interactions of original characteristics portfolios (solid) and PCs (dashed). Panel (a) focuses on the SDF constructed from PCs of interactions of 50 anomaly portfolios. Panel (b) shows coefficient estimates corresponding to PCs based on interactions of WFR portfolios. Dotted lines depict -1 s.e. bounds of the CV estimator.

results for the raw portfolio returns, it is apparent that a substantial degree of sparsity is now possible for both the anomalies and the WFR portfolios without deterioration in the OOS R^2. Strengthening the L^1-penalty to the point that only around 100 of the characteristics and their powers and interactions remain in the SDF (out of 1,375 and 3,400, respectively) does not reduce the OOS R^2 as long as one picks the L^2-penalty optimal for this level of sparsity. As before, an L^1-penalty-only approach leads to poor OOS performance.

The plots in the bottom row show contour maps for PCs. These results are drastically different from the ones in the top row in terms of how much sparsity can be imposed without hurting OOS performance. Very few PCs—or even just one—suffice to obtain substantial OOS explanatory power. But here, too, the combination of sparsity with an optimally chosen L^2 penalty is very important. Adding more PCs does not hurt as long as substantial L^2 shrinkage is imposed, but it does not improve OOS performance much either.

The two plots in Figure 4.6 take a cut in the contour plots along the ridge of maximal OOS R^2 from bottom to top, where we vary sparsity and choose the L^2 optimal shrinkage for each level of sparsity. These plots reinforce the point we noted from the contour plots that many of the powers and interactions of the characteristics are not adding pricing-relevant information to the SDF and can be omitted. The SDF that attains the highest OOS R^2 is relatively sparse with about 100 factors for both the anomalies on the left-hand side and the WFR portfolios on the right-hand side. However, as the wide standard error bands show, statistical precision is quite low. The very large number of portfolios in this case pushes the method to its statistical limits.

Overall, these results show that many of the powers and interactions of characteristics seem to be redundant in terms of their pricing implications. A majority of them can be excluded from the SDF without adverse impact on OOS pricing performance. But as before, L^2-shrinkage is crucial for obtaining good OOS performance.

4.4   OUT-OF-SAMPLE ASSET PRICING TESTS

Our cross-validation method evaluates a model's performance on the part of a sample not used in the estimation of the SDF coefficients; it is, therefore, by construction an OOS metric. Yet our choice of the strength of regularization (L^1 and L^2 penalties) is based on the entire sample. It is possible that the penalty that is optimal within one sample does not generalize well on new or fully withheld data. To address this potential issue, we now conduct an OOS test with a sample withheld from penalty estimation. Using our L^2-penalty method, we conduct the entire estimation, including the choice of penalty, based on data until the end of 2004. Post-2004 data is completely left out of the estimation. We then evaluate performance of the estimated SDF in the 2005–2017 OOS period. This analysis also allows us to assess the statistical significance of our earlier claim that characteristics-sparse SDFs cannot adequately describe the cross-section of stock returns.

This OOS exercise further helps to gain robustness against the effects of data mining in prior published research. Especially for the data set of 50 known anomalies, there is a concern that the full-sample average returns may not be representative of the ex ante expected returns of these largely ex-post selected portfolios. Implicitly, our analysis so far has already employed some safeguards against data mining bias. For data-mined spurious anomalies, there is no economic reason why their average returns should be related to exposures to high-variance PCs—and if they are not, our L^2 and dual-penalty specifications strongly shrink their contribution to the SDF. Even so, an OOS test on a fully withheld sample of post-2004 data provides additional assurance that the results are not unduly driven by data-mined anomalies.

Our analysis is very much in the spirit of Barillas and Shanken (2018) in that we compare the Sharpe ratios of the MVE portfolios implied by competing factor models (rather than the alphas of some "test assets"), albeit with an OOS focus. We proceed as follows. We first orthogonalize all factor portfolio returns with respect to the market using market betas estimated in the pre-2005 sample.[9] Given the estimate $\hat{b}$ based on our L^2-penalty Bayesian method in the pre-2005 sample, we construct the time series of the implied MVE portfolio $\hat{b}'f_t$ in the 2005–2017 OOS period. We focus on three sets of portfolios in constructing an SDF: the 50 anomaly portfolios, the 80 WFR portfolios, and the interactions and powers of 50 anomaly characteristics.[10] As in our earlier estimation, we choose penalties by three-fold cross-validation (two-fold if interactions are included) but with shorter blocks because we only use the pre-2005 sample here.

We then estimate abnormal returns of this OOS-MVE portfolio with respect to three characteristics-based benchmarks: the capital asset pricing model (CAPM); the six-factor model of Fama and French (2016) (with five cross-sectional factors, including the momentum factor); and our dual-penalty model where we have set the L^1 penalty such that the SDF contains only five cross-sectional characteristics-based factors. To compare the models on equal footing, we construct the MVE portfolio implied by these benchmarks. Since we work with candidate factor returns orthogonalized to the market return, the benchmark in the CAPM case is simply a mean return of zero. For the Fama-French six-factor model, we estimate the unregularized MVE portfolio weights, $\hat{w} = \overline{\Sigma}_f^{-1}\bar{f}$, from the five nonmarket factors in the pre-2005 period.[11] We then apply these weights to the five factor returns in the OOS period to construct a single benchmark return. Finally, for the dual-penalty sparse model with five factors, we estimate $\hat{b}$ in the pre-2005 period and then apply these optimal portfolio weights to returns in the OOS period. If our earlier claim is correct that the SDF cannot be summarized by a small number of characteristics-based factors, then our OOS-MVE portfolio constructed from the full set of candidate factors should generate abnormal returns relative to the MVE portfolio constructed from these sparse benchmarks.

[9] The resulting abnormal returns are $F_{i,t} = \tilde{F}_{i,t} - \beta_i R_{m,t}$, where $\tilde{F}_{i,t}$ is the raw portfolio return and $R_{m,t}$ is the market portfolio return. In our previous analysis, we used the full data to estimate β_i.

[10] We do not report results for interactions of WFR portfolios due to issues in estimating covariances in an even shorter sample with an extremely high number of characteristics-based factors in this case.

[11] As before, we orthogonalize these factors (SMB, HML, UMD, RMW, CMA) with respect to the market using factor loadings estimated in the pre-2005 sample.

TABLE 4.1

MVE portfolio's annualized OOS α in the withheld sample (2005–2017)

The table shows annualized alphas (in %) computed from the time-series regression of the SDF-implied OOS-MVE portfolio's returns (based on L^2-shrinkage only) relative to four restricted benchmarks: CAPM, Fama-French six-factor model, optimal sparse model with five factors, and optimal PC-sparse model with five PC-based factors. MVE portfolio returns are normalized to have the same standard deviation as the aggregate market. Standard errors are in parentheses.

SDF factors Benchmark	CAPM	FF 6-factor	Char.-sparse	PC-sparse
50 anomaly portfolios	12.35	8.71	9.55	4.60
	(5.26)	(4.94)	(3.95)	(2.22)
80 WFR portfolios	20.05	19.77	17.08	3.63
	(5.26)	(5.29)	(5.05)	(2.93)
1,375 interactions of anomalies	25.00	22.79	21.68	12.41
	(5.26)	(5.18)	(5.03)	(3.26)

Table 4.1 confirms that the MVE portfolio implied by our SDF performs well in the withheld data. The table presents the intercepts (alphas) from time-series regressions of the OOS-MVE portfolio returns on the benchmark portfolio return in percentage, annualized, with standard errors in parentheses. To facilitate interpretation of magnitudes, we scale MVE portfolio returns so that they have the same standard deviation as the market index return in the OOS period. The first column shows that the OOS-MVE portfolio offers a large abnormal return relative to the CAPM for all three sets of candidate factor returns. For example, for the OOS-MVE portfolio based on the 50 anomalies, we estimate an abnormal return of 12.35%, which is more than two standard errors from zero, despite the short length of the evaluation sample. The abnormal returns are even larger for the other two sets of portfolios. As the second column shows, the abnormal returns are very similar in magnitude for the FF six-factor model, and we can reject the hypothesis of zero abnormal returns at a 5% level or less for two of the three sets of candidate factor portfolios. The third column shows that the results for the sparse five-factor model based on our dual-penalty method is almost identical to the FF six-factor model. Overall, the evidence in this table confirms our claim that characteristics-sparse models do not adequately describe the cross-section of expected stock returns.

In our earlier analysis, we also found that sparse models based on PCs do much better than sparse characteristics-based models. This result also holds up in this OOS analysis. The last column shows that the PC-sparse MVE portfolio, which includes only five optimally selected PC-based factors using our dual-penalty method, performs uniformly better than characteristics-sparse models. Abnormal returns are much smaller and not statistically significantly different from zero for 80 WFR portfolios and only marginally significant for 50 anomaly portfolios.

4.5 RELATED RECENT RESEARCH

ML applications in cross-sectional asset pricing are currently a very active area of research. A number of recent papers use supervised learning techniques and offer insights that relate to the issues discussed in this chapter.

One line of work modifies principal components analysis (PCA) to impose, as in the SDF estimation in this chapter, economically motivated links between first and second moments of returns. Lettau and Pelger (2018) propose a variant of PCA where the factor extraction puts weight not only on explaining comovement, but also on explaining mean returns. Kelly, Pruitt, and Su (2019) use instrumented principal components (IPCA) to perform dimensionality reduction of the firm characteristics space. This method extends projected-PCA (Fan, Liao, and Wang 2016) by letting assets' loadings on latent factors depend on a vector of characteristics. IPCA then allows simultaneous estimation of latent factors and the parameters that relate characteristics to factor loadings. To implement this method, a researcher needs to pre-specify the number of latent factors. One can think of this preselection of a few dominant sources of covariance as pricing factors as a crude way of imposing the prior beliefs that high Sharpe ratios are more likely to come from major sources of covariances than from low-eigenvalue PCs. Rather than imposing a PC-sparse SDF representation ex ante, the method we discussed in this chapter automatically recovers such sparsity if it improves out-of-sample performance.

Freyberger, Neuhierl, and Weber (2020), Han, He, Rapach, and Zhou (2019), and Feng, Giglio, and Xiu (2020) focus on lasso-style estimation with L^1-norm penalties. They find a substantial degree of sparsity, suggesting substantial redundancy among cross-sectional stock return predictors. Yet, the results in this chapter suggest that, for the purposes of SDF estimation with characteristics-based factors, a focus purely on factor selection with L^1 penalty is inferior to an approach that includes an L^2 penalty that can shrink SDF coefficients toward zero to varying degrees without imposing sparsity on the SDF coefficient vector. This is in line with evidence from the statistics literature that lasso does not perform well when regressors are correlated, and that ridge regression (with squared L^2-norm penalty) or elastic net (with a combination of L^1 and L^2 penalties) delivers better prediction performance than lasso in these cases (Tibshirani 1996; Zou and Hastie 2005; see also our discussion of the issue in Section 2.2.1).

The analysis in this chapter allowed for simple forms of nonlinearity through characteristics interactions and powers of characteristics. A number of papers explore more sophisticated approaches in dealing with nonlinearity. Kozak (2019) builds on the approach in this chapter by employing regularization mapped into economic restrictions and SDF estimation, but using the *kernel trick* method to extend the set of characteristics to a potentially infinite-dimensional set of nonlinear functions of the original characteristics. Gu, Kelly, and Xiu (2020b) extend the ICPA approach of Kelly, Pruitt, and Su (2019) by using an autoencoder neural network method that allows factor loadings to depend nonlinearly on characteristics. Feng, Polson, and Xu (2018), Chen, Pelger, and Zhu (2019), and Gu, Kelly, and Xiu (2020a) also study neural networks to allow for nonlinearities. An interesting finding that emerges from the latter two papers is that the most important nonlinearities appear to be those arising from interactions between characteristics rather than nonlinearity in individual characteristics. This is consistent with the gains from including characteristic interactions that we saw in Table 4.1 in this chapter.

Moritz and Zimmermann (2016) and Bryzgalova, Pelger, and Zhu (2019) use tree-based approaches to entertain nonlinearity. Trees offer a natural generalization of conventional characteristics-sorted portfolios to allow for interactions between characteristics, but avoiding the curse of dimensionality. An important question in applying these methods to asset pricing is how to prune, or otherwise regularize, trees. Ideally, one would like to bring in economically interpretable restrictions, as we did in this chapter through the penalty function. Bryzgalova, Pelger, and Zhu (2019) tackle this problem by pruning and shrinking the tree based on a penalized mean-variance optimization problem similar to the one we employed in this chapter.

For interpreting the economic significance of the return predictability captured by these ML methods, it is useful to know to what extent the return predictability derives from stocks that are small and illiquid. To some degree, it is to be expected that predictability-inducing mispricings are bigger in the small-stock segment that attracts little interest by large investment managers. But economic significance would be substantially diminished if most or all of the profits of an ML-based strategy came from this segment. This is why the micro-cap stocks were completely excluded from analysis in this chapter and in many of the studies cited above, too. Avramov, Cheng, and Metzker (2019) examine more broadly the sensitivity of various ML-based portfolio returns to transaction costs and illiquidity. Another approach to dealing with illiquidity and transaction costs is to explicitly include transaction-cost optimization in the ML problem. DeMiguel, Martin-Utrera, Nogales, and Uppal (2019) find that doing so can increase the number of relevant characteristics under lasso-style estimation with L^1-norm penalty.

4.6 CONCLUDING REMARKS

This chapter showed that ML tools have natural applications in research on the cross-section of stock returns. Given the huge number of firm characteristics that seem to have cross-sectionally predictive information, the ML toolbox allows researchers to embrace the high dimensionality of this setting rather than artificially impose sparsity with ad hoc selected variables in small-scale models.

At the same time, the results in this chapter, and elsewhere in the recent literature, further underscore that cross-sectional asset pricing applications are quite different from typical ML applications in other fields. Nonlinearities play a more limited role than elsewhere in the ML space. Studies using neural networks and tree-based methods point toward characteristics interactions as a relevant form of nonlinearity, but other types of nonlinearities seem less important.

Unlike in many other ML applications, sparsity also seems limited. There is not a lot of redundancy in the predictive content of different firm characteristics. For some data sets—e.g., the ones in this chapter where we include an extremely large number of interactions and powers of stock characteristics—allowing for sparsity can help eliminate some useless factors, but the number of relevant characteristics is still very large. The multi-decade quest in the empirical asset pricing literature to summarize the cross-section of stock returns with sparse characteristics-based factor models containing only a few (e.g., three, four, or five) characteristics-based factors therefore seems futile.

Given the low signal-to-noise ratio in asset returns, an extremely flexible and purely data-driven approach to return prediction seems unlikely to succeed. Within the analysis in this chapter, injecting a modest dose of economic reasoning helped obtain a better-performing estimator. Formulating the approach in a Bayesian framework provided an avenue to bring in economically motivated reasoning in the choice of prior beliefs. We derive our particular L^2-penalty specification from an economically plausible prior that existence of near-arbitrage opportunities is implausible, and major sources of return co-movement are the most likely sources of expected return premia. As Kozak, Nagel, and Santosh (2020) discuss in more detail, modifying the prior beliefs toward specifications that are less well motivated by economic considerations would result in worse predictive performance. One interesting challenge for future research is to investigate whether one can also develop economically motivated approaches to regularization and hyperparameter estimation in other ML methods such as neural networks, trees, and random forests.

Chapter 5

ML AS MODEL OF INVESTOR
BELIEF FORMATION

In the previous chapters, we took the perspective of a statistician studying historical asset price data ex post. The statistician uses the ML toolbox to extract predictable patterns from the data with the objective of constructing useful asset return forecasts. In these analyses, we took the asset price data as exogenously given. The statistician was purely an outside observer with no effect on market prices.

If an outside observer of financial market data is confronted with a high-dimensional set of potential predictors, surely the investors in financial markets whose trading activity generated the price data face a similar high-dimensional prediction problem. For example, to value a stock, investors must forecast cash flows over multiple horizons stretching out many years into the future. The set of variables that could potentially have predictive information for these cash flows is immensely large. This set includes accounting data, textual information in the firm's periodic reports, the firm's announcements about plans and projects, industry conditions, macroeconomic variables, and so on.

Yet, existing asset pricing models do not put investors in such complex environments. In fact, most standard models assume rational expectations, which means that investors are assumed to already know the model generating the cash flows, including the values of the model's parameters. In other words, the problem of learning the predictive relationship between observed covariates and future cash flows has been assumed away. This assumption that investors have precise knowledge of the model and its parameters seems untenable once we consider the complexity of the environment in which actual real-world economic agents must solve forecasting problems. There is a literature in asset pricing and macroeconomics in which rational economic agents learn from observed data about parameters and model specification, and possibly the behavior of other agents. But the learning problem agents face in these models is typically low-dimensional. This understates the difficulty of the agents' learning problem.

One may therefore wonder whether empirical properties of investors' forecasts and decisions that seem anomalous from the perspective of standard models of rational belief formation could actually be a consequence of the oversimplification of the learning problem in these models. For example, in the large "factor zoo" in empirical cross-sectional asset pricing that we looked at in the previous chapter, could it be that some of these return predictability patterns in historical data are actually a consequence of investor learning about the predictive content of these variables? Is there perhaps a connection between the rapid growth in recent decades of the set of potential predictors of stock fundamentals that are observable to investors and the growth in the number of variables that researchers have found to predict returns (Harvey, Liu, and Zhu 2016)?

The ML methods we have reviewed in the previous chapters provide an attractive blueprint for modeling investor learning in high-dimensional environments. ML methods not only deal with the complexity of the learning environment in a sophisticated way, without artificially forcing the learning problem to be low-dimensional, but they also have some resemblance to the statistical methods that sophisticated quantitative investors use in the real world. Thus, rather than using the ML tools to analyze data ex post, we can let investors inside a theoretical model use them to learn about the world and to price assets.

In this chapter, I discuss some basic steps toward an asset pricing model in which investors face a high-dimensional learning problem. The material in this chapter is a simplified version of the analysis presented in Martin and Nagel (2019). Investors in this model use a set of covariates to forecast firm cash flows and they price stocks based on these forecasts. To make these forecasts, investors have to estimate the functional relationship between the covariates and future cash flows from observed historical data. That investors face this learning problem has a profound effect on asset price properties, especially when the number of potentially relevant predictor covariates is large relative to the number of stocks that generate the historical data that investors learn from.

Investors' learning problem in this model is, in many ways, still an overly simplified representation of the learning problem faced by real-world investors. For example, the set of relevant predictor variables is known, the functional form of the predictive relationship is linear and known (only parameters need to be learned), and the stochastic process that generates stock fundamentals is time-invariant. Moreover, investors in this model optimally digest the available information without frictions. For this purpose, they use the Bayesian regression tools we discussed in the previous chapters. Keeping investors' problem simple and their belief formation statistically optimal has the effect of minimizing the estimation errors investors make when they learn about the cash flow process.

Even so, when an econometrician applies standard return predictability tests to returns generated in this economy, returns appear predictable in ways that resemble the effects of risk premia and investor behavioral biases, despite the fact that neither risk premia nor behavioral biases exist in this model. The high dimensionality of investors' learning problem changes the equilibrium properties of asset prices. When investors' learning problem is low-dimensional, returns are close to being martingale differences from the econometrician's viewpoint. But under high dimensionality, this is no longer the case.

The relatively simple linear environment with known functional forms is a good starting point for analyzing these questions, but it still leaves unexplored many questions of how investors form beliefs about value-relevant variables in a more complex environment. Studying investor learning with ML methods that are suitable for nonlinear settings with unknown functional forms may offer additional insights into asset price behavior in financial markets. The next chapter will offer some thoughts on directions that future research could take in exploring these questions.

5.1 The Asset Market

I begin by laying out the environment in which investors learn about the process that generates asset cash flows. There are N assets and time is discrete, $t \in \{1, 2, ...\}$. Each asset is associated with J firm characteristics observable to investors that we collect in the $N \times J$ matrix X. We assume that $\text{rank}(X) = J$, so none of the characteristics are redundant, and that firm characteristics are normalized such that $\frac{1}{NJ} \text{tr} X'X = 1$.

The assets pay dividends, collected in the vector y_t. Dividend growth, $\Delta y_t = y_t - y_{t-1}$, is partly predictable based on the firm characteristics X:

$$\Delta y_t = Xg + e_t, \quad e_t \sim N(0, I_N). \tag{5.1}$$

The matrix X contains all variables that investors can condition on in forecasting dividend growth. This cash flow specification is, in many ways, still much simpler than the cash flow process that real-world investors have to learn about.

First, the relationship between cash flow growth and characteristics is linear, and we assume investors know that it is linear. In reality, there are likely to be nonlinear relationships between covariates and future cash flow growth. But this assumption is not as limiting as it may seem as one could accommodate nonlinearity in this specification by including nonlinear functions of characteristics in the matrix X.

Second, we assume that the matrix X is constant over time. In reality, firms' characteristics change. To some extent, we could accommodate this in our setting by thinking of y_t as a vector of payoffs for hypothetical characteristics-constant firms. This means that we would have to reshuffle the actual firms each period so that each element of y_t is always associated with the same characteristics. What our framework does not allow for is a change over time in the cross-sectional moments of the characteristics in X. With a stochastically changing X it could happen, for example, that two characteristics that are highly correlated in one period are no longer strongly correlated in future periods. This would make investors' learning and forecasting problems harder.

Third, while we consider a fairly high-dimensional environment in with J can be close to N, we assume that $J < N$. The set of characteristics available to real-world investors is potentially very large and so $J \geq N$ might be reasonable. An extension to allow for $J \geq N$ would be relatively straightforward, but at the cost of considerably greater notational complexity. The effects of learning on asset price properties can be seen more clearly in the simpler $J < N$ setting.

Overall, our model therefore likely understates the difficulty of the learning problem that actual investors face in their investment decision-making process. Even so, as analysis in this chapter will show, the properties of asset prices are strongly affected by learning. Extending the model to take into account realistic additional complications in the learning problem would further enhance these effects.

The properties of the parameter vector g, and investors' beliefs about the values of these parameters, play an important role in our analysis. Specifically, the magnitudes of the elements of g determine the proportion of cash flow growth variation that is predictable with X. Therefore, when investors learn about g from historical observations of Δy, the magnitudes of the g elements determine the ratio of signal (variance of Xg) to noise (variance of e) in Δy.

We assume that the vector g is drawn from a multivariate normal distribution,

$$ g \sim \mathcal{N}\left(0, \frac{\theta}{J} I_J\right), \tag{5.2} $$

where θ is a constant. We think of g as drawn by nature, at the very beginning of this economy, before any dividends are realized and any assets priced. It then stays constant through time. The specification of variances and covariances as proportional to $1/J$ in (5.2) ensures that the signal to noise ratio is invariant to J. To see this, note that if investors had perfect knowledge of the parameter vector g, investors would be able to fully predict the Xg component of Δy_t in (5.1). One can show that this predictable component has the cross-sectional variance $\frac{1}{N} \mathbb{E}[g'X'Xg] = \theta$.[1]

---

[1] Apply the trace operator, use its cyclical properties, and use the normalization of $\text{tr}(X'X) = NJ$ from above.

5.1.1 Investors

Investors are homogeneous and risk-neutral. We further assume that the interest rate is zero. This means that return predictability cannot be a consequence of risk premia or time-varying interest rates. By abstracting from risk premia, we intentionally make it easy for an econometrician to test market efficiency in our setting. Since risk premia are absent, there is no joint hypothesis problem due to unknown risk pricing models. Yet, as we will show, the presence of investors' learning problem still makes interpretation of standard market efficiency tests tricky.

Homogeneity of investors is a simplifying assumption. As a first cut to this problem, we want to keep the analysis as transparent as possible. But this is not to say that heterogeneity is unimportant. It would be interesting and realistic to extend the setting to allow for heterogeneity, perhaps with investors differing in their methods of data analysis or in the data that they observe. Heterogeneity would also introduce the possibility of investors having to learn about the models and beliefs of other investors. Such learning about endogenous objects could potentially introduce additional interesting asset price dynamics. In this analysis here, however, we want to first see to what extent asset price properties change when we introduce learning and high dimensionality in a homogeneous investor setting.

5.1.2 Pricing

To keep the asset valuation simple, we focus on the pricing of one-period dividend strips, i.e., the claim to a single dividend one period ahead. The vector p_t represents the prices, at time t, of claims to dividends that will be paid at time $t + 1$. This focus on dividend strips is not as restrictive as it may seem. One can think of one period in this model as a long time span, say a decade, and the dividend strip payoff as the cash flows of a long-lived stock compressed into a single cash flow that occurs at the typical duration of a stock.

Given risk neutrality and zero interest rate, p_t is then equal to the investors' expectation of next-period dividends,

$$p_t = \widetilde{\mathbb{E}}_t y_{t+1} = y_t + \widetilde{\mathbb{E}}_t \Delta y_{t+1} = y_t + \widetilde{\mathbb{E}}_t \left(Xg + e_{t+1} \right) .$$

The issue of central interest in this chapter is how investors form these expectations $\widetilde{\mathbb{E}}_t [\cdot]$.

As a benchmark, consider the case of rational expectations where investors are assumed to know g. In this case, there is no learning problem. Dividend expectations are constant at $\widetilde{\mathbb{E}}_t \left(Xg + e_{t+1} \right) = Xg$. Prices under rational expectations therefore are

$$p_t = y_t + Xg, \tag{5.3}$$

and realized price changes, which we refer to from now on as "returns," are

$$r_{t+1} = y_{t+1} - p_t = \Delta y_{t+1} - Xg = e_{t+1}. \tag{5.4}$$

The ultimate goal of our analysis is to understand how investors' belief formation affects the properties of asset prices. In particular, we are interested in finding out whether belief formation based on learning could induce return predictability. In the existing asset pricing literature, return predictability in the cross-section of stock returns is commonly attributed to the presence of risk premia or behavioral biases of investors. But here we want to see whether learning in a high-dimensional environment could be an alternative source of return predictability.

5.1.3   An Econometrician Observer

For this purpose, we consider an econometrician who observes the assets' realized returns in this economy. The econometrician uses these returns to run standard regression-based return predictability tests. More precisely, the econometrician asks whether the firm characteristics X can be used to predict returns in the cross-section. Regressing realized returns on characteristics, the econometrician obtains the vector of coefficients:

$$b_{t+1} = (X'X)^{-1} X' r_{t+1}. \tag{5.5}$$

In the case of investors with rational expectations in (5.4), where $r_{t+1} = e_{t+1}$, returns are unpredictable and

$$b_{t+1} = (X'X)^{-1} X' e_{t+1}. \tag{5.6}$$

Any deviations from zero of the elements of b_{t+1} are purely due to estimation error, induced by noise e_{t+1} that ended up, by chance, having some correlation with the columns of X. This is the null hypothesis that underlies a vast literature on market efficiency tests and cross-sectional stock return anomalies. Given that the elements of e_{t+1} are distributed $\mathcal{N}(0, 1)$, it would follow, under this null, using the usual OLS variance formulas (with known residual variance), that

$$\sqrt{N} b_{t+1} \sim \mathcal{N}\left(0, N(X'X)^{-1}\right), \tag{5.7}$$

which provides the basis for standard significance tests in return predictability regressions.

For a test of the null that all elements of h_{t+1} are jointly zero, one can form a statistic that would have a χ^2 distribution under the rational expectations null hypothesis:

$$h'_{t+1}X'Xh_{t+1} \sim \chi_J^2. \tag{5.8}$$

This quadratic form is also, at the same time, measuring the return of a portfolio that weights stocks based on in-sample predicted returns,

$$w_t = \frac{1}{N}Xh_{t+1}. \tag{5.9}$$

With these weights, the portfolio return is

$$r_{IS,t+1} = w'_t r_{t+1} = \frac{1}{N}h'_{t+1}X'Xh_{t+1}. \tag{5.10}$$

An important point to emphasize—and one that we will come back to—is that this portfolio is an in-sample trading strategy. The portfolio weights use information that real-time investors would not have at the beginning of period $t+1$ because the portfolio weights depend on the regression coefficients h_{t+1} that are estimated from $t+1$ returns. Hence, a decision maker restricted to using only data available in real time would not be able to construct these return predictions at the beginning of period $t+1$. Similarly, tests based on the statistics (5.7) and (5.8) are tests of in-sample, not out-of-sample return predictability.

In the rational expectations case, the distribution (5.8) implies that if the econometrician were to repeatedly sample from this economy, in expectation the portfolio would have the return

$$\mathbb{E}\, r_{IS,t+1} = \frac{J}{N}. \tag{5.11}$$

Under rational expectations, prices are martingales and returns are unpredictable, in-sample and out-of-sample. The expected value of $r_{IS,t+1}$ is greater than zero purely because of in-sample overfitting of noise. Just as one needs to adjust R^2 measures for in-sample overfitting, one needs to compare this portfolio return to the χ^2-distribution in (5.8) rather than zero in order to test the rational expectations null.

Rejections of the null based on test statistics like (5.8) are typically interpreted as an indication that some combination of risk premia and behavioral biases of investors must be present. But when investors are not endowed with perfect knowledge about g and must estimate it from observed historical data, it is not clear that this interpretation is valid. For this reason, we now analyze what happens to the properties of return predictability tests when the econometrician applies these tests to asset price data from an economy in which investors must learn about g from observed historical data.

5.2 INVESTOR LEARNING

To learn about g from historical data, investors apply statistical analysis. At every point in time, they use the cash flow growth data available until this point to estimate g. In principle, there is a wide variety of statistical methods, including the nonlinear ML methods that we discussed in previous chapters, that investors might rely on for this purpose. But here we assume that investors know that there is a linear relationship between the firm characteristics in X and cash flow growth, as specified in (5.1). Given this knowledge, investors will run linear regressions to estimate g. However, as we will see now, there are still additional choices we need to make within the category of linear regression methods in order to fully pin down investors' belief formation mechanism.

5.2.1 OLS Learning

As a heuristic approach to the learning problem, we could assume that investors simply run OLS regressions. Since applied statistical analyses by forecasters and analysts often use OLS regression, this approach is not only simple, but also has intuitive appeal. As we will see, though, in a high-dimensional environment, we will need to apply some modifications to obtain a plausible model of investor belief formation. But OLS learning is a good starting point before we introduce these modifications.

Since cash flow growth in (5.1) is IID, historical data over t periods can be summarized by the sample average

$$\overline{\Delta y}_t = \frac{1}{t} \sum_{s=1}^{t} \Delta y_s, \tag{5.12}$$

and a pooled cross-section and time-series regression of cash flow growth on X is equivalent to a regression of $\overline{\Delta y}_t$ on X:

$$\tilde{g}_{OLS,t} = (X'X)^{-1} X'\overline{\Delta y}_t. \tag{5.13}$$

This model of learning is a cross-sectional analog to the time-series learning models in Lewellen and Shanken (2002) and Timmermann (1993). The Lewellen-Shanken model is a special case of the OLS learning model here with a single asset and X reduced to a scalar equal to 1.

If investors form expectations based on the OLS estimates $\tilde{g}_{OLS,t}$, then $\tilde{\mathbb{E}}_t \Delta y_{t+1} = X\tilde{g}_{OLS,t}$ and we get equilibrium prices

$$p_t = y_t + X\tilde{g}_{OLS,t}, \tag{5.14}$$

and realized returns

$$
\begin{aligned}
r_{t+1} &= y_{t+1} - p_t \\
&= X(g - \tilde{g}_{OLS,t}) + e_{t+1}.
\end{aligned}
\tag{5.15}
$$

From the investors' viewpoint at time t, the expectation of g is equal to $g_{OLS,t}$. As a consequence, investors perceive returns as unpredictable, as in the rational expectations case earlier.

However, from the viewpoint of an econometrician who can observe data before and after period t, the returns in (5.15) appear predictable. The source of this predictability is a component in realized returns that is induced by investors' estimation error $g - \tilde{g}_{OLS,t}$ when estimating g. Using the fact that $\tilde{g}_{OLS,t} = Xg + X\left(X'X\right)^{-1} X'\bar{e}_t$, where $\bar{e}_t = \frac{1}{t} \sum_{s=1}^{t} e_s$, we can write the realized returns as

$$r_{t+1} = -X(X'X)^{-1}X'\bar{e}_t + e_{t+1}. \tag{5.16}$$

Written this way, we see how the noise, $\bar{e}_t$, in historical average dividend growth generates the estimation error that then contaminates realized returns: by chance, the columns of X have some degree of correlation with $\bar{e}_t$. This pushes $\tilde{g}_{OLS,t}$ away from g, prices away from the rational expectations prices in (5.3), and returns away from e_{t+1}. As a consequence, when the econometrician regresses realized returns in period $t+1$ on X, the regression coefficients are different from those in the rational expectations case (5.6). The econometrician obtains

$$b_{t+1} = - \left(X'X\right)^{-1} X'\bar{e}_t + \left(X'X\right)^{-1} X'e_{t+1}. \tag{5.17}$$

Compared with the rational expectations case in (5.6), there is now an additional term on the right-hand side. This additional term arises from the estimation error component of realized returns in (5.16).

Now consider again, as in the rational expectations case, a portfolio with weights $w_t = \frac{1}{N}Xb_{t+1}$ based on in-sample predicted returns from the regression in (5.17). In this case, the expected value of the portfolio return

$$r_{IS,t+1} = w_t'r_{t+1} = \frac{1}{N}b_{t+1}'X'Xb_{t+1} \tag{5.18}$$

is

$$
\mathbb{E}\, r_{IS,t+1} = \frac{1}{N}\, \mathbb{E} \left[\bar{e}'_t X \left(X'X \right)^{-1} X' \bar{e}_t \right] + \frac{1}{N} \left[e'_{t+1} X \left(X'X \right)^{-1} X' e_{t+1} \right]
$$

$$
= \frac{J}{tN} + \frac{J}{N}. \tag{5.19}
$$

If the econometrician adjusts $\mathbb{E}\, r_{IS,t+1}$ for the expected return under the rational expectations null (5.11) by subtracting J/N, this still leaves the term $\frac{J}{tN}$. If J is very small relative to N, this term may be negligibly small. However, in the high-dimensional case, when J is comparable in magnitude to N, the econometrician will find that this in-sample trading strategy has a substantial positive expected return in excess of the rational expectations benchmark. Accordingly, if the econometrician compares the realized value of $r_{IS,t+1}$ to the χ^2-distribution in (5.8) that the portfolio return would have under the rational expectations null, she will likely find that $r_{IS,t+1}$ is far in the tail of this distribution.

In this model, unlike in a rational expectations setting, it would be incorrect to conclude that a finding of $\mathbb{E}\, r_{IS,t+1} > J/N$ indicates that risk premia exist or that investors must have behavioral biases. In this model, investors are risk neutral and hence risk premia are zero. Investors also do not have behavioral biases (with the caveat that we still have to evaluate whether OLS learning is the optimal learning approach here). The economic explanation is different: the first term in (5.19) that generates the high expected returns relative to the rational expectations benchmark is a consequence of investor learning about g.

For example, when a firm characteristic (a column of X) happens to be positively correlated with $\bar{e}_t$ in the sample investors observe up to time t, then investors will end up being too optimistic, relative to the rational expectations benchmark, about stocks with a positive value of this characteristic. Hence, their price is too high, and future returns are low. The opposite is true for stocks with low values of this characteristic. An econometrician with access to $t+1$ return data can then pick up this in-sample return predictability by regressing r_{t+1} on this characteristic.

While OLS learning has intuitive appeal due to its widespread use of OLS regressions in applied statistics and forecasting, it is an ad hoc approach. It is not clear that this is the optimal learning approach for investors in this setting. And if it is not the optimal approach, could it be that the in-sample return predictability that arises with OLS learning is just a consequence of investors using a suboptimal approach?

5.2.2 Bayesian Learning with Informative Prior

The optimal approach for rational investors to learn about g is to apply Bayesian updating. To implement Bayesian updating, we need to specify the prior beliefs that investors hold about the distribution of g before seeing any cash flow data. We assume that this distribution is multivariate normal:

$$g \sim \mathcal{N}(0, \Sigma_g). \tag{5.20}$$

That prior beliefs are centered around zero means that investors a priori, before seeing any data, don't know which characteristics predict cash flow growth by how much and in which direction. This seems plausible. But what about the prior covariance matrix Σ_g? We assume that Σ_g is proportional to the identity matrix so that all the predictor variables are on an equal footing from the prior perspective. The remaining task then is to specify the proportionality constant. A conservative assumption—in the sense that it minimizes investors' estimation errors that then show up as predictable components in returns—is that investors' prior is objectively correct: we give investors the knowledge of the true distribution in (5.2) from which the elements of g are actually drawn. Investors' prior covariance matrix therefore is $\Sigma_g = \frac{\theta}{J}I_J$, and hence prior beliefs are

$$g \sim \mathcal{N}\left(0, \frac{\theta}{J}I_J\right). \tag{5.21}$$

In this framework, with normally distributed sources of uncertainty, and a linear cash flow generating process (5.1), Bayesian updating implies that investors' posterior mean is given by the Bayesian regression estimator (2.22) that we discussed in Section 2.4:

$$\tilde{g}_t = \left(X'X + \frac{J}{\theta t}I_J\right)^{-1} X'\overline{\Delta y_t}. \tag{5.22}$$

Using an eigendecomposition $\frac{1}{N}X'X = Q\Lambda Q'$, where $\Lambda = \mathrm{diag}(\lambda_1, ..., \lambda_J)$ and Q is an orthogonal matrix of eigenvectors, we can rewrite the posterior mean as the OLS estimator shrunk by a shrinkage matrix Γ_t,

$$\tilde{g}_t = \Gamma_t (X'X)^{-1} X'\overline{\Delta y_t}, \tag{5.23}$$

where the symmetric matrix Γ_t takes the form

$$\Gamma_t = Q\left(I_J + \frac{J}{N\theta t}\Lambda^{-1}\right)^{-1} Q'. \tag{5.24}$$

Shrinkage is a consequence of the informative prior for g. To see explicitly what the degree of shrinkage depends on, note that $\left(I_J + \frac{J}{N\theta t}\mathbf{\Lambda}^{-1}\right)^{-1}$ is diagonal with elements

$$\frac{\lambda_j}{\lambda_j + \frac{J}{N\theta t}}$$

along its diagonal. Thus shrinkage is strong if t or θ are small, or J/N is large, or along principal components with small eigenvalues. In these cases, the prior's influence on the posterior is strong because the observed data is not very informative relative to the prior.

The derivations above outline the mechanics of Bayesian updating. But there is an important underlying economic interpretation. Economic plausibility calls for an informative prior in which the prior covariance parameter θ is not extremely large so that the elements of g cannot be arbitrarily big. Extremely big g would imply that the cross-sectional variance of the predictable component of cash flow growth, Xg, is huge relative to the variance of unpredictable noise e. This would mean that most of cash flow growth variation is predictable based on firm characteristics—which is not a plausible representation of economic reality. For this reason, it makes economic sense for investors to believe, a priori, that extremely large magnitudes of g are unlikely.

This also makes clear why OLS learning lacks economic plausibility in this setting. OLS learning arises as the special case in which the prior is diffuse, with $\theta \to \infty$. In this case, $\mathbf{\Gamma}_t$ converges to an identity matrix and $\tilde{g}_t$ to the OLS estimator. Having investors learn with OLS therefore effectively assumes that investors ignore that extremely large magnitudes of predictable cash flow growth components are economically implausible.

In a low-dimensional setting where J/N is very small, this would not matter much. As we can see from the expression in (5.24), $\mathbf{\Gamma}_t$ converges to an identity matrix if $J/N \to 0$ and hence the posterior mean converges to the OLS estimator. OLS learning may therefore be a fine as a model of investor belief updating in a low-dimensional setting.

But if J is close to N in magnitude, the situation is very different. In this case, there is a big wedge between the OLS estimator and the posterior mean in (5.23). OLS learning would not only be economically implausible in this case, but it would also lead to poor forecast performance. Figure 5.1 illustrates this. It shows the mean-squared error in investors' forecasts of Δy_t when investors have observed, and learned from, one period of cash flow realizations Δy_{t-1}. For this example, we set $J = 900$, $N = 1000$, the elements of X are drawn independently from a standard normal distribution, and the vector g is drawn from the prior distribution (5.21) with $\theta = 0.5$. The solid line shows the mean-squared error

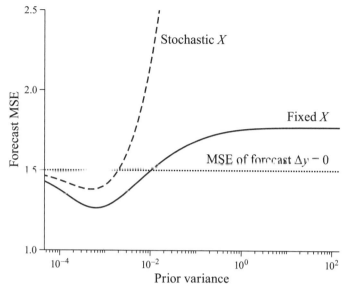

Figure 5.1. Cash flow forecast mean-squared error

$$MSE = \frac{1}{N} \left[\Delta y_t - X\tilde{g}_{t-1}(\theta)\right]' \left[\Delta y_t - X\tilde{g}_{t-1}(\theta)\right]$$

when investors entertain different values for θ in their prior.

The case where investors form prior beliefs based on $\theta = 0.5$ is the case in which they have an objectively correct prior. In this case, the prior variance θ/J is approximately 5.6×10^{-4}. This is where the forecast MSE reaches its minimum in Figure 5.1. OLS learning would be the limit with $\theta \to \infty$ and hence prior variance going to infinity. As the figure shows, going in this direction worsens the forecast performance. In fact, when investors' prior variance is substantially higher than the variance of an objectively correct prior, there is a point where the forecast MSE is higher than the forecast MSE of a random-walk forecast that simply sets the estimated g to zero and forecasts $\Delta y_t = 0$. The MSE of this random-walk forecast is shown as the dotted line. This illustrates how poorly a forecast based on a diffuse prior performs when J is big.

Figure 5.1 shows another interesting variation where we let the X matrix be stochastic. We redraw the elements of X each period. Cash flows are then generated as $\Delta y_t = X_{t-1}g + e_t$. Investors regress Δy_{t-1} on X_{t-2} to learn about g. To forecast Δy_t they then apply these estimates to X_{t-1}. The dashed line in Figure 5.1 shows the resulting forecast MSE. The minimum is still the same as in the fixed-X case: the objectively correct prior minimizes the forecast MSE. However, the deterioration in forecast performance with an excessively dispersed prior is much worse in this case. OLS forecasts would produce extremely inaccurate predictions.

Intuitively, the reason is that when the number of covariates, J, is close in magnitude to the number of observations, N, many columns of X will end up, by chance, highly positively or negatively correlated, even though their elements are IID.[2] OLS tends to assign very large coefficient magnitudes to such highly correlated pairs of covariates that are largely offsetting each other in the OLS fitted value. The OLS objective function is almost flat regarding these coefficients. Small coefficient magnitudes or large coefficients that make the covariates mostly cancel each other in the OLS fitted value produce almost the same fit. If the covariate matrix X remains fixed, they also largely offset in the forecast based on the OLS estimates. OLS having difficulty pinning down the magnitudes of these coefficients therefore does little harm. However, if the covariate matrix changes stochastically, it is likely that a pair of covariates that was, just by chance, highly correlated in X_{t-2} is no longer highly correlated in X_{t-1}. As a consequence, the huge OLS coefficient estimates obtained from regressing on X_{t-2} no longer have offsetting effects in the forecast that applies these estimates to X_{t-1}. This contaminates the forecast with a huge estimation error and results in poor forecast performance.

With an informative prior close to the objectively correct prior this problem is ameliorated because, as we mentioned above, shrinkage is particularly strong along principal components of $\frac{1}{N}X'X$ with small eigenvalues. Small eigenvalues exist if some characteristics are approximately spanned by other characteristics. The posterior mean then strongly downweights contributions to the forecast that come from covariates that have close to offsetting effects in the OLS estimates.

That X is drawn independently every period may be too extreme as a representation of stochastically changing firm characteristics, but an autoregressive process with a certain degree of persistence may be realistic. For the rest of this chapter, we stick to the case of fixed X. But it is useful to keep in mind that a stochastic X would make investors' forecasting problem more difficult and would further enhance the importance of informative prior beliefs.

5.3 RETURN PREDICTABILITY

We now examine the properties of returns when investors price assets based on the posterior in (5.23) that results from objectively correct,

---

[2]In other words, $\frac{1}{N}X'X$ will have a substantial number of small eigenvalues. Asymptotically, if $N \to \infty$ and J/N converges to a fixed constant, the distribution of eigenvalues of $\frac{1}{N}X'X$ follows the Marchenko-Pastur distribution.

informative prior beliefs. Compared to returns under OLS learning in (5.15), there is now an additional term in the expression for returns:

$$r_{t+1} = X(I_J - \Gamma_t)g - X\Gamma_t(X'X)^{-1}X'\bar{e}_t + e_{t+1}. \tag{5.25}$$

The first term on the right-hand side of (5.25) appeared because of the shrinkage induced by the informative prior. With diffuse prior, and hence OLS learning, we would have $\Gamma_t = I_J$ and the term would disappear. But with informative prior it is nonzero. We can interpret this term as the effect of "underreaction," due to shrinkage, to the fundamental information in X.

As in the OLS learning case, the second term represents the effect of noise on investors' posterior mean. The purpose of shrinkage induced by the informative prior is to dampen the effects of this noise-induced estimation error. Shrinkage via Γ_t dampens this component, but at the cost of generating the first term. Under Bayesian learning, Γ_t optimally trades off the pricing error arising from these two components.

5.3.1 In-Sample Return Predictability

When an econometrician samples returns from this economy and regresses the returns in (5.25) on X, then the expression for the regression coefficients, as the one for returns in (5.25), now has an additional term compared with the OLS learning case:[3]

$$b_{t+1} = (X'X)^{-1}X'r_{t+1}$$
$$= (I_J - \Gamma_t)g - \Gamma_t(X'X)^{-1}X'\bar{e}_t + (X'X)^{-1}X'e_{t+1}. \tag{5.26}$$

The first term on the right-hand side is a consequence of the first term in the return expression (5.25). Shrinkage induced by the informative prior leaves this component in returns that is correlated with the columns of X. Consequently, it gets picked up in the regression of returns on X.

Now let's revisit the in-sample portfolio strategy with weights $w_t = \frac{1}{N}Xb_{t+1}$, using b_{t+1} from (5.26). In this case, results in Martin and Nagel (2019) show that the expected value of the portfolio return $r_{IS,t+1} =$

---

[3] One could also let the econometrician use shrinkage methods like ridge regression, effectively imposing a prior that the coefficients in the return predictability regression cannot be too big. If the econometrician's prior distribution of the coefficients is roughly in line with the true distribution of the coefficients, using such methods would strengthen the in-sample return predictability, but it would not qualitatively change the results.

$w'_t r_{t+1} = b'_{t+1}(X'X)b_{t+1}$ is

$$\mathbb{E}\, r_{IS,t+1} = \frac{1}{N}\,\mathbb{E}\left[g'(I_J - \Gamma_t)'X'X(I_J - \Gamma_t)g\right]$$

$$+ \frac{1}{N}\,\mathbb{E}\left[\bar{e}'_t X\,(X'X)^{-1}\,\Gamma_t X'X\Gamma_t X'\bar{e}_t\right] + \frac{1}{N}\left[e'_{t+1}X\,(X'X)^{-1}\,X'e_{t+1}\right]$$

$$= \frac{1}{N}\sum_{j=1}^{J}\left(\frac{\lambda_j}{t\lambda_j + \frac{J}{N\theta}} + 1\right). \tag{5.27}$$

When $\theta \to \infty$, this expression converges to the expected return we obtained in the OLS learning case in (5.19).

To interpret the magnitudes, it is useful to note that since $r_{IS,t+1} = \frac{1}{N}b'_{t+1}X'Xb_{t+1}$, the expected return $\mathbb{E}\, r_{IS,t+1}$ also represents the expected total explained return variance in the in-sample predictive regression, while $1 - J/N$ is the variance of the residual. We can therefore construct an adjusted R^2 measure from the return prediction regression,

$$R^2_{adj.} = 1 - \left(1 - \frac{\mathbb{E}\, r_{IS,t+1}}{1 - J/N + \mathbb{E}\, r_{IS,t+1}}\right)\frac{N}{N - J}. \tag{5.28}$$

In the rational expectations case $\mathbb{E}\, r_{IS,t+1} = J/N$, as we showed in (5.11), and hence this adjusted R^2 is exactly zero. With learning, however, there are in-sample predictable components in returns that raise $R^2_{adj.}$ above zero.

Figure 5.2 illustrates this with a numerical example. As before, $N = 1000$ and we draw IID elements of X from a standard normal distribution. The vector g is drawn from the prior distribution (5.21) with $\theta = 1$. As Martin and Nagel (2019) discuss, with $\theta = 1$, the share of predictable variation in cash flow growth is roughly of the same magnitude as the share of long-term earnings growth rates over a 10-year horizon that are forecastable with analyst forecasts according to the evidence in Chan, Karceski, and Lakonishok (2003). If we interpret one period in the model as a 10-year time window, we get an empirically realistic cross-section of cash flow growth rates. We set $t = 1$, which means that investors have learned from one period of cash flow growth observations.

The solid line in Figure 5.2 shows the adjusted R^2 for different values of J. When J is not small relative to N, the adjusted R^2 is substantially above zero. For example, with $J = 900$, the adjusted R^2 is above 25%. In other words, an econometrician running this regression would find substantial in-sample return predictability even though investors in this economy do not demand any risk premia and they do not have behavioral biases in their belief formation.

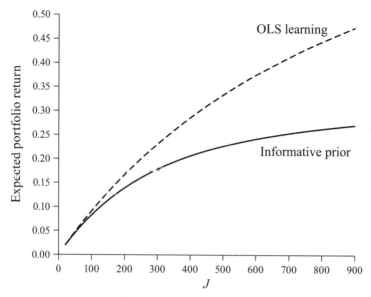

Figure 5.2. Adjusted R^2 in in-sample return prediction regression

The dashed line shows that in-sample return predictability would be even stronger under OLS learning. By imposing shrinkage based on an objectively correct prior, investors can avoid excessive contamination of asset prices and returns with estimation error from their learning about g. Doing so minimizes the amount of in-sample return predictability, but it cannot eliminate it.

Martin and Nagel (2019) further look at the properties of formal statistical tests of return predictability. Under the hypothesis of rational expectations—the null hypothesis in a large number of empirical studies of the cross-section of stock returns—returns are $r_{t+1} = e_{t+1}$ and hence unpredictable. This in turn implies the null hypothesis that the true values of the regression coefficients b_{t+1} in (5.26) are zero. To analyze the properties of tests of this null, Martin and Nagel apply high-dimensional asymptotics where $N \to \infty$ and $J \to \infty$ at the same time, with J/N converging to a fixed constant. This type of asymptotic analysis delivers a closed-form solution for the asymptotic distribution of test statistics, but unlike conventional fixed-J, large-N asymptotics, it ensures that J does not vanish in magnitude relative to N so that investors' learning problem remains relevant. This is important because the asymptotic results are meant to approximate the properties of statistical tests in a finite-sample case where the number of covariates is not small relative to N and investors therefore remain uncertain about the parameter vector g. Martin and Nagel show that a test of the rational expectations null hypothesis rejects with probability 1 in the asymptotic limit. Furthermore, this result holds for any fixed t, i.e., even if investors have learned about g from data spanning many periods.

Overall, an econometrician studying the returns in a large-J/N economy is likely to come away with the conclusion that returns are predictable by the firm characteristics in X. The typical conclusion from empirical rejections of the no-predictability null in in-sample tests is that models of risk premia or mispricing due to imperfectly rational investors are needed to explain the evidence. But the analysis here shows that when J is not small relative to N, in-sample predictability tests lose their usual economic meaning because there is a third possibility: in-sample return predictability arises because investors' forecasting problem is high-dimensional. Investors' estimation errors contaminate returns and they look, ex post, predictable.

5.3.2   (Absence of) Out-of-Sample Return Predictability

The analysis in this chapter has so far focused on in-sample predictability tests. In these tests, the fit of the return prediction regression is evaluated on the same sample of returns that was used to estimate the coefficients in this regression. Investors making decisions in real time, without the benefit of hindsight, would not be able to exploit the predictability captured in these regressions. The econometrician looking at an in-sample regression estimated ex post therefore uses information that investors did not have when they priced assets.

To put the econometrician on the same footing with investors, we now look at out-of-sample (OOS) predictability. We consider the returns on a portfolio $r_{OOS,t+1} = w'_{OOS,t} r_{t+1}$, where the weights applied to $t+1$ returns are based on regression coefficients estimated from time t returns:

$$w_{OOS,t} = \frac{1}{N} X h_t. \tag{5.29}$$

This is a portfolio strategy that would be implementable in real time.

Martin and Nagel (2019) show that $\mathbb{E} r_{OOS,t+1} = 0$. Thus, even in the high-dimensional case where investors have to learn about the predictive role of a large number of firm characteristics, there is no OOS return predictability. This is an intuitive result. Since investors are Bayesian, they use available information optimally. Moreover, we endowed them with an objectively correct prior. Once we put the econometrician on the same footing as investors by preventing use of look-ahead information that investors do not have, the econometrician can no longer predict investors' forecast errors and asset returns.

Therefore, researchers interested in empirically isolating risk premia or behavioral biases of investors should focus on OOS predictability, not in-sample predictability. In a low-dimensional setting, with J small, this would not be a big issue. But in a high-dimensional setting there is a big wedge between in-sample predictability, which picks up learning-induced investor forecast errors, and out-of-sample predictability.

The OOS tests do not need to be true OOS tests (like those, for example, in McLean and Pontiff (2016)) where the researcher has to wait, after formulating a hypothesis, until a sufficient amount of new, yet-unstudied data has been produced. The result that $\mathbb{E} r_{OOS,t+1} = 0$ also applies to pseudo-OOS tests where the econometrician obtains return data ex post but makes sure that the regression coefficients used to weight $t + 1$ returns are estimated only with data that was available at time t. The result that $\mathbb{E} r_{OOS,t+1} = 0$ applies to such a pseudo-OOS strategy, too. Of course, this assumes that there are no other complications present that are not captured in the model and that could invalidate the pseudo-OOS test. For example, if a researcher today can go back in time and construct variables in historical data that were not available to investors at the time when they priced assets, then the prediction $\mathbb{E} r_{OOS,t+1} = 0$ does not hold for pseudo-OOS trading strategies based on such variables.

Martin and Nagel (2019) further show that the pseudo-OOS test could also be performed backward in time where the weights in (5.29) that use regression coefficients estimated from returns at time t (or later) are applied to returns at $t - 1$, i.e., $w'_{OOS,t} r_{t-1}$. This backward OOS portfolio return, too, has expected return of zero in this model. This is not a tradable strategy, but potentially interesting for econometric practice as it supports an alternative route for pseudo-OOS return predictability tests. The fact that many cross-sectional asset pricing anomalies do not hold up in backward OOS tests (Linnainmaa and Roberts 2018) could therefore indicate that these anomalies are not due to risk premia or behavioral biases, but rather the consequence of investor learning in a high-dimensional environment.

The absence of backward OOS predictability is also interesting because it provides support for cross-validation methods we discussed in earlier chapters. When data is partitioned into estimation and validation samples, some validation blocks will temporally precede some of the estimation blocks. Therefore, if a researcher wants to train an ML algorithm to predict cross-sectional differences in asset returns due to risk premia or OOS exploitable mispricing, but does not want the algorithm (e.g., during hyperparameter optimization) to pick up in-sample predictability induced by investor learning, then for cross-validation to work, it must be true that learning does not introduce backward OOS return predictability.

Martin and Nagel (2019) add a note of caution, though. The absence of forward-OOS return predictability is a natural, and likely a general property of Bayesian learning (with objectively correct prior), but the backward result might be somewhat specific to the environment in this model. It is still an open question how general the absence of backward OOS predictability result is.

5.4   EXTENSIONS

The basic modeling framework can be extended in a number of interesting directions that may bring further realism to the model. This section briefly reviews two of these directions: sparsity in investors' cash flow forecasts and extra shrinkage or sparsity. Both of these can be understood as modifications of the prior beliefs that investors approach the learning problem with.

5.4.1   Sparsity

The stochastic environment we have assumed so far leads investors to apply shrinkage in their cash flow forecasting regressions, but they do not impose sparsity. But it may be plausible that investors also use sparsity to discipline their forecasting models in a high-dimensional environment. By changing distributional assumptions, we can obtain a sparse solution in investors' learning problem that still remains close to, but not exactly equal, to the Bayesian posterior mean. We need that, (i) investors' prior is that the elements g_j of g are drawn from a Laplace distribution,

$$f(g_j) = \frac{1}{2b} \exp\left(-\frac{|g_j|}{b}\right),$$

where $2b^2 = \frac{\theta}{J}$ is the variance; and (ii) investors price assets based on the mode rather than the mean of the posterior distribution (i.e., based on a MAP estimator). In this case, investors' forecasts can be represented as the fitted values from a Lasso regression (Tibshirani 1996).

That investors use the posterior mode in pricing is a deviation from the fully Bayesian framework. As a consequence, the result that the expected OOS portfolio return in (5.29) is zero no longer holds exactly. In simulations, Martin and Nagel (2019) show that the deviations are small, and overall, the return predictability looks very similar to the shrinkage without sparsity case.

5.4.2   Extra Shrinkage or Sparsity

In the Bayesian framework we used in this chapter so far, shrinkage (or sparsity) in investors' cash flow forecasting model is purely a consequence of investors' informative prior beliefs. Given these prior beliefs, it is statistically optimal to regularize the forecasting model. Moreover, the prior was objectively correct so that the extent of shrinkage was not only optimal given investors' subjective beliefs about the cash flow process, but it was also optimal in light of the actual process.

Statistical optimality considerations are not necessarily the only reason why investors may force shrinkage or sparsity on their forecasting models. One simple economic reason for sparsity can be that variables are costly to observe. In this case, investors face a trade-off between the forecasting benefits of this variable and the cost of observing it. For costly-to-observe variables, it may not be worth including them in the forecasting model if the benefit does not exceed the cost. Relatedly, investors may perhaps prefer sparse models with fewer predictor variables because of a desire to keep the forecasting model simple and interpretable. One could micro-found such a desire for simplicity as boundedly rational limited attention as in Sims (2003), Gabaix (2014), and Molavi, Tahbaz-Salehi, and Vedolin (2020). In these models, agents employ shrinkage and sparsity to minimize the cost of attention.

We can introduce such additional motives for shrinkage and sparsity in our framework by making investors' prior beliefs concentrated more tightly around zero than under the objectively correct prior (where the prior distribution agrees with distribution that we draw g from in generating the data). In this case, the result that the OOS portfolio return in (5.29) is zero no longer holds. Martin and Nagel (2019) show that the OOS portfolio return is positive in this case. Intuitively, investors now underweight the information in X about cash flow growth. As a consequence, there is a component in returns that is predictable with X not only in- but also out-of-sample.

Figure 5.3 illustrates this with simulated OOS portfolio returns. We use the same parameter values as in Figure 5.2. The dotted line show the expected OOS portfolio return in the case of an objectively correct prior. Consistent with our arguments earlier, it is zero for all values of J. Recall that that the covariance matrix of the objective prior is $\Sigma_g = \frac{\theta}{J}I$. If θ in investors' prior is replaced with $\theta/2$, shown by the dashed line, or $\theta/4$, shown by the solid line, the OOS expected portfolio return is positive and increasing in J. The excessively tight prior distribution induces excessive shrinkage and OOS predictable components in returns. In a model with Laplace prior and sparsity, the effects of excess shrinkage are very similar to the ones shown in Figure 5.3.

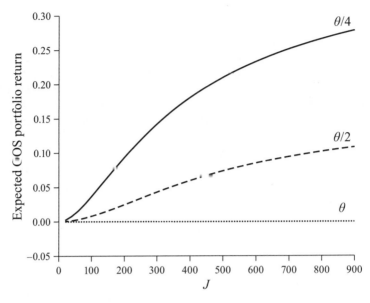

Figure 5.3. Expected OOS portfolio return when investors learn with excessive shrinkage

Therefore, if a researcher empirically finds OOS return predictability, one possible interpretation is that excessive shrinkage or sparsity in investors' cash flow forecasting models is the underlying cause. When the number of potentially relevant predictors is large, the influence of the prior beliefs on the posterior mean is strong and a relatively small amount of tightening of the prior distribution relative to an objective prior can produce substantial OOS return predictability.

5.5   Implications for Empirical Research

The analysis in this chapter has shown that the properties of the cross-section of stock returns are sensitive to the dimensionality of the environment in which investors price stocks. The basic assumption that investors face a high-dimensional prediction problem when they forecast firms' cash flows is arguably realistic. In this environment, investors end up making forecast errors that look predictable ex post in in-sample regressions on cash flow relevant covariates. These forecast errors contaminate returns, making returns predictable as well. When investors deal with this high dimensionality in a sophisticated way by employing

Bayesian regression shrinkage rather than, say, simple OLS regression, they minimize this return predictability, but they cannot eliminate it.

These results raise questions about the interpretation of empirical research in cross-sectional asset pricing. Some empirical studies in this area econometrically test asset pricing models. Others search for new factors or return predictors. The vast majority of this empirical work looks at the data, implicitly or explicitly, through the lens of rational expectations models in which investors are assumed to know the relevant parameters of the processes generating asset fundamentals. Under this null hypothesis, in-sample regressions run ex post on historical data consistently estimate the return predictability that investors see ex ante. Hence, the conclusion follows that such in-sample return predictability must reflect either risk premia or systematic mistakes investors make when pricing assets. The results reviewed in this chapter cast doubt on this interpretation. When investors face a high-dimensional environment, in-sample return predictability evidence loses the economic content it has in a rational expectations setting. While the rational expectations model may be a good approximation when investors' environment is low-dimensional and hence learning only has small effects on asset prices, it is no longer a good approximation in the high-dimensional case. In-sample predictability can be the consequence of investors not having precise knowledge of the parameters of a data-generating process that involves large numbers of potentially relevant predictor variables.

Put differently, the economic content of the (semi-strong) market efficiency notion that prices "fully reflect" all public information (Fama 1970) is not clear in a high-dimensional setting. Researchers usually emphasize the "joint hypothesis problem" as the main difficulty in interpreting market efficiency tests: the econometrician studying asset prices does not know the model that determines risk premia required by risk-averse investors. But even leaving aside this problem, the interpretation of the market efficiency notion is not clear. Does "fully reflect" mean that investors know the parameters of the cash flow prediction model or, alternatively, that investors employ Bayesian updating when they learn about these parameters? The analysis in this chapter shows that there is a big wedge between these two interpretations. The former, adopted in much of the empirical literature, can be tested with in-sample return predictability regressions. In a setting in which investors face a high-dimensional environment, this does not seem like an economically interesting hypothesis. Its rejection does not warrant the conclusion that risk premia must be presented or that investors must be subject to behavioral biases that induce mispricing.

This suggests an alternative interpretation of the "factor zoo" in the cross-section of stock returns (Cochrane 2011; Harvey, Liu, and Zhu

2016). Much of the evidence in this literature is based on in-sample predictability tests. Empirical discoveries of new cross-sectional return predictors in such in-sample tests are less interesting once we recognize that investors have to digest the predictive information of a large number of forecasting variables. A world in which researchers have at their disposal such a large array of candidate return predictors is also one in which investors have to consider many of the same variables as candidate predictors of cash flows. In this world, in-sample return predictability evidence does not tell us much about the expected returns that investors perceived on ante at the time they priced assets.

To differentiate between learning-induced predictability on one hand and risk premia and mispricing on the other, we need evidence from OOS tests. True OOS tests are often not feasible and researchers will have to rely on pseudo-OOS tests, emulating real-time forecasting ex post on historical data. From the perspective of the model in this chapter, pseudo-OOS tests are just as good as true OOS tests.[4] Alternative evidence that supports the economic underpinnings of a risk premium or behavioral bias theory from perspectives other than return prediction regressions, e.g., with data on macroeconomic risk exposures or investor expectations, can also be helpful in making the case that an in-sample predictable component of returns is not an artifact of investors' learning process. In a high-dimensional environment, such alternative perspectives are particularly valuable.

Some papers in the "factor zoo" literature already report pseudo-OOS return predictability results. One example is the last part of the previous chapter where we discussed OOS predictability. The evidence indicates that OOS returns are not zero. But there is a substantial decay in return predictability from in- to out-of-sample. Efforts to build models of risk premia or of systematic, persistent investor biases should focus on such OOS robust cross-sectional return predictability patterns.

Looking at the world through the lens of rational expectations models, empirical researchers are often skeptical of OOS testing. Under the rational expectations hypothesis, where investors do not face a learning problem, in- and out-of-sample return predictability tests examine the same hypothesis. And in-sample tests are more powerful because they use the available data to the fullest extent. Therefore, it is not clear why one would want to focus on OOS tests (Inoue and Kilian 2005; Campbell and Thompson 2008; Cochrane 2008, Hansen and Timmermann 2015). But

---

[4]Of course, only if done without p-hacking, multiple testing, and data mining (Lo and MacKinlay 1990; Harvey, Liu, and Zhu 2016; Chordia, Goyal, and Saretto 2019). Pseudo-OOS return predictability tests can be subject to these distortions just like in-sample tests.

viewed from the perspective of learning models, the situation is different. If investors face a high-dimensional learning problem, in- and out-of-sample tests examine fundamentally different hypotheses. Learning can generate in-sample predictability, but not OOS predictability. OOS tests therefore have a clear economic motivation.

Finally, the results in this chapter also provide a perspective on how technological progress in data construction and data analysis could affect the return predictability observed in empirical research. Many cross-sectional stock return studies use historical data from time periods in which investors had less data available at their fingertips and much more constrained data processing capabilities than researchers have today. Researchers can easily construct variables today (say, through automated textual analysis of corporate filings) that were basically inaccessible to investors several decades ago even though the data may have existed in principle (e.g., in the form of hardcopy annual reports). Through the lens of the model in this chapter, we can interpret this lack of data access as forcing investors to employ excessively sparse valuation models when they priced assets. Following the logic of the analysis in Section 5.4.2, it is therefore likely that when researchers use current methods and technology to construct predictor variables in earlier historical time periods, these variables predict returns not only in in-sample, but also in pseudo-OOS tests. For variables that may not have been available to investors when they priced assets, researchers should be cautious in attributing the return predictability to risk premia or behavioral biases of investors.

5.6 CONCLUDING REMARKS

This chapter has shown how the presence of a high-dimensional learning problem in investors' cash flow forecasting has important effects on the statistical properties of asset prices. As the availability of data that is potentially relevant for investors' cash flow forecasting keeps expanding, these learning-induced pricing effects are likely to grow in importance.

We developed these ideas within a cross-sectional asset pricing framework, but they are likely much more broadly relevant. Similar issues arise in any setting in which economic agents learn to make forecasts and face a potentially large number of relevant predictors. The statistical properties of forecast errors will be sensitive to the dimensionality of investors' learning problem. Forecast error predictability that seems anomalous relative to a rational expectations benchmark could be a consequence of learning in a high-dimensional environment.

The next chapter outlines directions that research on investor learning in complex environments could take in the future. This discussion includes some thoughts on how the ideas in this chapter could be applied in other economic settings. The next chapter also offers suggestions for extending the analysis of learning effects beyond the simple linear Bayesian regression framework toward a model in which economic agents deal with more challenging ML problems in their forecasting and decision making.

Chapter 6

A RESEARCH AGENDA

THE NUMBER OF ML applications in asset pricing is growing rapidly. This parallels similar growth in many other areas of economics where ML methods are quickly becoming part of the standard toolkit, such as, for example, in causal inference (Athey and Imbens 2019) and for textual analysis (Gentzkow, Kelly, and Taddy 2019). ML methods hold promise for advancing our understanding of asset prices. Empirically, they permit the study of the relationships between asset prices and a rich set of information without forcing artificial and ad hoc sparsity on the empirical models. In theoretical studies, ML tools can provide inspiration for modeling of economic decision making in settings with complex sources of uncertainty without imposing unrealistic simplicity on the environment.

Chapters 4 and 5 provided two examples of empirical and theoretical applications of ML approaches. These analyses, and other related recent studies, have produced some novel insights about the properties of asset prices. Embracing the high dimensionality of the prediction environment faced by investors leads to a richer empirical description of the investment opportunity set. It also helps, theoretically, to better understand how assets are priced in financial markets.

But many questions remain unanswered. To a large extent, the literature in this area is still in an early exploratory phase. Different papers apply different methods to similar problems, but there is no consensus yet on the most suitable ML methods for particular sets of problems in asset pricing. A central theme of this book is that off-the-shelf application of ML tools, without injecting some degree of economic reasoning, is unlikely to work well. Asset price data have specific properties that call for an ML approach that is tailored to these conditions. A lot of work remains to be done to integrate ML methods more firmly with asset pricing theory and existing empirical methods.

In this chapter, I discuss some of these research opportunities. This sketch of a research agenda is by no means a complete survey of open questions in this area, but I hope that it can serve as useful inspiration for future research. As in much of this book, I focus mostly on the cross-section of stock returns in my discussion of these research opportunities, but there are, of course, related potential applications in other areas of asset pricing as well.

I begin with empirical applications of ML tools. Part of the challenge in empirical work is to sort out how to select and tweak ML methods to be most useful in asset pricing applications. Some progress has been made, but many questions remain about economically appropriate methods of regularization, the role of nonlinearities, and how to deal with structural change in the underlying data-generating process.

While most of the recent ML applications in asset pricing have focused on return prediction or closely related tasks, ML methods could be useful for other purposes, too. I discuss two areas where application of ML methods seems promising. Both broadly fall into the area of asset demand analysis. One is the empirical estimation of asset demand systems from detailed investor portfolio holdings data; the other is the analysis of investor expectations data.

Finally, I offer some suggestions on how asset pricing theory could advance by adopting ML as a model of investor belief formation in high-dimensional environments. This discussion builds on the analysis in Chapter 5, which raised questions about how to conduct and interpret empirical work on return predictability. But the insights researchers have obtained so far may just be the tip of the iceberg. There are many directions in which one could take this approach further. There is more to be discovered about asset pricing from exposing investors within theoretical models to a realistically complex, high-dimensional environment in which learning is difficult.

6.1   Characterizing Investment Opportunities

Return predictability analyses, factor model estimation, and construction of empirical SDFs all help to characterize the investment opportunities available in financial markets. Given the richness of the information that is available to researchers for constructing predictors of returns and risks, this is a natural area for application of ML methods. Early work in this area has often taken tools off the shelf from elsewhere in the ML literature. Much work remains to be done to adapt ML tools for the specific conditions in asset pricing.

6.1.1   Economic Restrictions for ML

Given the low signal-to-noise ratio in asset price data, prior knowledge of the researcher plays a more important role than in other ML applications. An extremely flexible, purely data-driven approach is unlikely to work well. For this reason, it is important to fuse ML methods with economic restrictions that provide some a priori structure to guide the choice of ML algorithm, the method of regularization, and other aspects of the approach.

Chapter 4 illustrated how this can be done in a Bayesian regression setting. The Bayesian setting made it relatively straightforward to connect the estimation approach with economic restrictions. In this case, economically motivated restrictions like the absence of near-arbitrage opportunities and concentration of factor premia in major sources of return covariance can be imposed through the prior beliefs about SDF parameters.

This approach, however, completely abstracted from frictions. This potentially misses useful prior information about assets and portfolios that are most likely to exhibit big magnitudes of expected excess returns and Sharpe ratios. Short-sale constraints and other limits to "arbitrage" could cause such premia to be concentrated among assets where these frictions are particularly strong. Therefore, extending the prior beliefs specification to allow for friction-induced patterns in expected returns could potentially lead to further improvement in out-of-sample predictive power. For this purpose, one would need to relate the prior variance of expected asset returns to asset characteristics that predict the presence of frictions. This would reduce the degree of shrinkage that is applied to expected return estimates for assets that are likely affected by frictions.

It would also be interesting to build stronger bridges between structural economic models of asset prices (i.e., asset pricing models with explicit assumptions about investor beliefs and preferences) and ML approaches. With the Bayesian regression framework, this again should not be too complicated. One could tilt prior beliefs about expected returns or SDF parameters toward the predictions implied by structural asset pricing models. This would be somewhat similar in spirit to the approach in Pástor and Stambaugh (2000), but in a high-dimensional setting and with structural rather than reduced-form asset pricing models. An analysis along these lines would allow researchers to investigate whether imperfect, partially misspecified models could nevertheless have some value in describing the investment opportunity set.

A Bayesian regression approach makes it relatively easy to inject economic restrictions through prior beliefs. But there are many other interesting ML approaches that do not fit into the Bayesian regression framework. An important task for future research is to investigate whether one can combine economic reasoning with other ML methods, too. Bryzgalova, Pelger, and Zhu (2019) take some steps toward this goal for tree-based methods. They prune and shrink trees based on a penalized mean-variance optimization problem that is closely related to the criterion that we discussed in Chapter 4 within the Bayesian regression approach.

Can one find a similar connection to economic optimization criteria in neural network methods? Is it possible to give an economic interpretation of ensemble methods such as bagging and boosting? Answers to these questions would be a big step forward toward tightly integrating ML methods into the empirical asset pricing toolkit.

6.1.2 Nonlinearities

At several points in this book, I have conjectured that nonlinearities may play a less prominent role in asset pricing applications than in many typical ML applications outside of finance. This is not to say, however, that nonlinearities can be neglected. First, the focus of this book is on equity markets and on prediction problems that involve first moments of equity returns. Nonlinearities may play a bigger role in other areas of asset pricing. For example, in default risk modeling, nonlinearities are more prominent than in stock returns. This may give an edge to ML methods that are particularly well suited for accommodating these nonlinearities. Second, even in equity market research, certain types of nonlinearities seem relevant. Based on the evidence that the ML literature on the cross-section of stock returns has accumulated so far, first-order interactions between firm characteristics appear to be the quantitatively most important type of nonlinearity.

An interesting question that remains to be answered in this regard is whether nonlinear methods like neural networks and tree-based approaches actually have a clear advantage over linear penalized regression models (e.g., elastic net) that include covariate interactions. For example, the elastic net that Gu, Kelly, and Xiu (2020a) compare with neural networks does not include covariate interactions. It is clear that nonlinear methods outperform linear methods without interaction, but it is still an open question whether an elastic net approach that includes covariate interactions can perform as well as a neural net or tree-based approach in asset pricing applications. Sorting out this question would be a big help toward a better understanding of which of the many available ML methods are best suited for asset pricing applications.

Interpretability is a concern with nonlinear models. To give an economic interpretation of the predictive success of a model, we need to be able to assess how different covariates contribute to the predictions of the model. One can look at the gradient, but this provides only a local assessment of covariate influence around a particular value of the covariate vector. Recent research has made some progress on developing summary measures of the global influence of a variable. For example, Horel and Giesecke (2019) propose a statistic that is a weighted average of squared partial derivatives of a neural network estimator and that allows statistical significance testing. These issues are also relevant for asset pricing applications of nonlinear models. Along the lines of our discussion in Section 3.2, for economic interpretation it would be particularly useful to develop metrics that reveal how covariates contribute to the squared Sharpe ratio of a portfolio, or the variance of an SDF, constructed based on the predictions of the estimated network.

6.1.3   Structural Change

Perhaps the most important empirical challenge is to adapt ML methods for structural change in asset markets. Asset return moments change over time as the structure of the economy changes, investors learn from experienced history, the mix of market participants changes, and technology advances. Most ML methods are not designed for settings undergoing such continuous structural change. Accordingly, the existing ML papers in cross-sectional asset pricing have so far taken an approach that mostly neglects this structural change. As in standard rational expectations econometrics, they proceed, implicitly, under the assumption that there is an underlying stable law of motion generating returns that an econometrician can recover by sampling asset return data over relatively long periods.

As Chapter 5 made clear, this is a particularly unpalatable assumption in a high-dimensional environment. If a large number of covariates are available to an econometrician as potential return predictors, this also means that investors have to digest the predictive information from a large number of covariates. Learning these predictive relationships from observed data is subject to parameter uncertainty. As a consequence, realized asset returns may be contaminated with substantial estimation errors that were not predictable in real time to investors, but that may look predictable ex post to the econometrician in in-sample regressions. Moreover, to the extent that some variables truly predict returns in an out-of-sample sense—perhaps because learning is slower and more imperfect than in the frictionless Bayesian model of Chapter 5—this predictive relationship is likely to change over time. There may be a dynamic process of anomaly discovery and elimination by arbitrageurs.

In this sense, the advancement of ML-inspired methods in asset pricing has brought to the surface a tension that needs to be resolved. On one hand, empirical asset pricing research has pushed methods toward more realism by taking into account large numbers of predictors without imposing ad hoc sparsity on prediction models. On the other hand, once we recognize the high dimensionality of the environment investors operate in, the implicit assumption that the predictive role of these predictors for asset returns was stable over decades looks untenable. In rudimentary ways, this has already been addressed to some extent in many recent papers. The use of hold-out samples for pseudo-OOS tests and, in some cases, rolling estimation approaches, is basically an acknowledgement that predictive relationships may not be stable over time. Yet, there is so far no systematic treatment of the structural change issue in asset pricing ML studies.

Structural change complicates the application of ML approaches in several ways. In Section 3.8, we briefly discussed two of these complications. One is that structural change implies that not only parameters of the prediction model may change over time, but hyperparameters for example, penalty parameters in ridge regression or lasso—may change, too. Another one is that standard cross-validation methods for model validation and hyperparameter estimation that are indifferent to time ordering of observations lack justification when structural change is present. Drawing validation data from time periods that precede all or part of the training data is fine in a stationary setting, but may not be appropriate when there is structural change in the predictive relationships.

There are several directions in which future research could progress on this question. First, computational considerations loom large. Repeatedly retraining computationally demanding learners over largely overlapping rolling data sets is inefficient and may be prohibitively expensive for some ML methods. Finding computationally efficient updating schemes could help overcome this obstacle. In Section 3.8 we discussed that this is straightforward for ridge regression where the estimator can be expressed in a recursively updated form. For other methods, it is not as simple, but the literature offers some suggestions, too. For example, Angelosante and Giannakis (2009) and Monti, Anagnostopoulos, and Montana (2018) suggest recursive approaches for lasso. Martínez-Rego, Pérez-Sánchez, Fontenla-Romero, and Alonso-Betanzos (2011) propose an updating scheme for neural networks that allows for gradual forgetting of earlier data. Whether any of these approaches, perhaps with some modifications, could work well in asset pricing applications is not clear at this point, but it seems like an interesting direction to explore.

Second, as we did in Chapter 4 in a stationary setting, it seems important to develop a framework that allows us to link statistical approaches for handling structural change with economic principles. While computational efficiency considerations may dictate the choice of updating scheme in some applications, it would nevertheless be useful to understand what an updating scheme should look like, ideally, given some prior beliefs about the underlying economic model of asset prices and the reasons for structural change. For example, if the underlying economic model is one in which investors are learning from historical data about predictive relationships—e.g., as in Chapter 5 but perhaps with slower learning speed so that some OOS return predictability exists—this type of model may prescribe a particular form of parameter updating.

Third, once the appropriate tools for tracking structural change are in place, the ultimate goal is to use these tools to characterize the dynamics of OOS predictable asset returns. As Chapter 5 made clear, in a high-dimensional environment, the economic insights that can be obtained from in-sample return prediction regressions are rather limited. Returns are contaminated with learning-induced forecast errors that look predictable ex post in in-sample regressions. To isolate risk premia or the pricing consequences of behavioral biases of investors, we need to study OOS predictable returns.

The notion that there is structural change in the investment opportunity set and that anomalies apparent in historical data may not persist into the future is not a new idea. McLean and Pontiff (2016) is a prominent example of a recent paper that tries to quantify these changes. But econometric practice in empirical asset pricing mostly does not embrace this notion. For example, empirical work that looks for priced systematic risk typically does so with in-sample analyses. Similarly, tests of behavioral finance models typically use in-sample analyses. While some OOS analysis with hold-out samples may be present in some papers, dynamic learning processes and structural change are not front and center in much of the literature. Adapting ML methods to account for structural change would help to move away from this static perspective toward a more dynamic, continuously changing characterization of the investment opportunity set that is arguably a more realistic representation of how investors see the world in real time.

6.2 Asset Demand Analysis

ML methods are useful not only for analyzing asset price data—that is, market equilibrium outcomes—but also for understanding the underlying drivers of asset demand. I focus my discussion of research opportunities in this area on two complementary approaches that rely on different types of data. One looks at asset demand in a rather direct way by examining investor holdings data in a demand system estimation framework. The other is more indirectly connected to asset demand and looks at expectations of investors—or, as proxies, the forecasts of analysts and professional forecasters—that may be an underlying determinant of asset demand.

6.2.1   Demand System Estimation

Koijen and Yogo (2019) have introduced an asset demand system estimation approach to asset pricing. Similar to product demand estimation
in industrial organization research, asset demand in this framework has
two components. One part is a function of observable asset characteristics (such as market equity, book equity, profitability, and many other
characteristics commonly used in empirical asset pricing). The remainder
is latent demand that is due to asset characteristics that are unobservable
to the econometrician. The demand system can be estimated from portfolio holdings data for different groups of investors present in the market.
The estimated system provides price elasticities of asset demand that can
then be used, in conjunction with a market clearing condition, to conduct counterfactual exercises, such as, for example, to assess the effects
on asset prices of a shock to asset supply.

This approach to asset pricing comes with several empirical challenges
that ML methods can help address. First, the set of characteristics that are
potentially relevant for asset demand is likely extremely large. Koijen and
Yogo (2019) use a small number of characteristics and this leaves much
of asset demand attributed to latent demand. It would be interesting to
know whether this result changes when a much larger set of characteristics is considered with methods that are well suited for high-dimensional
estimation problems. As we discussed in Chapter 4, a large number of
characteristics are relevant for predicting cross-sectional differences in
stock returns. Within the asset demand system model, the characteristics
that explain variation in expected returns in equilibrium must be characteristics that determine investors' expectations of asset payoffs, or their
perceptions of risk, and hence their asset demands.

Second, there is a large degree of heterogeneity in the characteristics
that are relevant for different investors. A subset of characteristics that
matters for one group of investors may be ignored by other groups.
In other words, there may be substantial sparsity in investor-level asset
demand functions. ML methods may therefore be useful to allow for such
sparsity and to deal with it in a computationally efficient way.

Third, just as for asset return prediction, structural change is likely
important. It seems unrealistic that investors' asset demand functions
could stay stable over long periods of time. Therefore, adapting ML methods to handle structural change is likely to be useful for asset demand
system estimation as well.

Similar types of challenges arise in consumer product demand system
estimation. Accordingly, the literature there has started to adopt ML tools
to address these challenges. Athey and Imbens (2019) and Gillen, Montero, Moon, and Shum (2019) discuss approaches that can handle the

high dimensionality and sparsity of these settings. These methods may potentially be applicable in asset demand estimation, too.

6.2.2 Expectations Formation

Beliefs about asset returns are a potentially important determinant of asset demand and, ultimately, of equilibrium asset prices. Studying the properties of market participants' forecasts of asset returns—or of variables like earnings, GDP growth, and inflation that should be related to asset return expectations—can help shed light on the belief formation process. For many classes of investors, direct expectations data is not available. Empirical studies therefore examine expectations of professional forecasters or equity analysts as proxies for the unobservable investor expectations.

There is a huge literature on the properties of such forecasts. However, the typical benchmark in this literature is a model of rational expectations in which forecasters know the parameters of the underlying model generating the variables they are forecasting. Studies have used in-sample forecast error predictability regressions to document various empirical deviations from this benchmark, including over- or underreaction to surprise information.

In-sample tests of forecast error predictability are, however, subject to the same issues that we discussed in Chapter 5 for in-sample return predictability tests in high-dimensional settings. Recall that realized returns in the model in Chapter 5 are simply the errors in investors' forecasts of future asset payoffs. The in-sample return predictability arising in this model is really a manifestation of more general in-sample forecast error predictability under Bayesian learning. Forecasters' learning about the data-generating process contaminates forecast errors with error components that are in-sample predictable, although they are not predictable OOS.

There is therefore an opportunity to take a fresh look at the properties of expectations of investors, analysts, and macroeconomic forecasters with a different approach. The approach should account for the high dimensionality of forecasters' environment and it should evaluate forecasts against OOS benchmarks that do not give a look-ahead advantage to the econometrician the way in-sample tests do. Disentangling learning-induced estimation errors from belief distortions due to bounded rationality and behavioral biases is an important step toward a better understanding of expectations formation in financial markets and the macroeconomy.

The ML methods reviewed in this book provide the tools to accomplish this. They allow researchers to construct forecast benchmarks that take into account the predictive information in a large number of potentially relevant covariates that are observable to forecasters. Combining this large amount of predictive information in a regularized and, possibly, sparse and nonlinear model, researchers can built a benchmark that represents how a highly sophisticated forecaster would form expectations.

Just as in asset return prediction, structural change is an important issue for forecast benchmarking, too. The relationship between observable covariates and the variables to be forecasted is unlikely to be stable over long periods of time. To be a good representation of how a skilled forecaster would build a forecasting model, an ML-based forecast benchmark should account for such structural change. Rolling-window estimation is a simple possibility, but, as we discussed earlier in this chapter, there may be better approaches.

Bianchi, Ludvigson, and Ma (2020) is a recent example of research that follows this path. They examine professional forecasts of macroeconomic variables. Their forecast benchmark accommodates high dimensionality through a dynamic factor model and regularization. The forecasts from this benchmark are based only on information that is available to forecasters in real time with model training and validation conducted with a rolling window approach.

6.3   THEORY APPLICATIONS OF ML

Empirical work in asset pricing has started to embrace the notion that prediction problems are high-dimensional and that empirical methods should be able to handle this high dimensionality. There are many promising opportunities to do the same in theoretical modeling of financial markets. Chapter 5 showed that theory-implied properties of asset prices are very different, and in some ways closer to empirical reality, when investors' high-dimensional learning problem is not assumed away. Much more research remains to be done—in asset pricing, and in economics more generally—on models in which economic agents confront a complex reality with the tools of a statistician, and in which, like a real-world statistician, they are left with considerable uncertainty about the laws of motion governing the world.

The analysis in Chapter 5 stayed, on purpose, within a Bayesian frictionless framework and thus very close to existing learning models in asset pricing. We wanted to introduce high dimensionality into investors' learning without at the same time also introducing any other costs, constraints, and imperfections. But this is not to say that these complications are not relevant. The frictionless Bayesian setting is a useful starting point, but it makes investors' learning problem still, in many ways, too easy. In this section, I discuss a few ideas about how to enrich such models so that they better represent the complexity that investors face in the real world and how they deal with it.

6.3.1 Bounded Rationality

Once we admit that investors operate in a complex environment in which they have to keep track of a large number of predictor variables, it also becomes hard to defend the assumption that there are no bounds to rationality. Gathering large amounts of data may require costly search, acquisition, and processing. Computational capacity may be limited. In addition, decision makers may have a preference for tractable, simple, and transparent models.

In Chapter 5 we took a small step in this direction when we explored the consequences of excessive shrinkage or sparsity in investors' forecasting models. This can be thought of loosely as a consequence of a cost of model complexity or a preference for simpler models. However, we did not microfound this deviation from the frictionless Bayesian model. A related example is the model in Molavi, Tahbaz-Salehi, and Vedolin (2020). Theirs is a time-series setting in which investors use an excessively sparse factor model to make forecasts and price assets.

Much work remains to be done to understand better how frictions shape the data sets and models that investors work with. Some potentially useful ideas already exist in recent work. For example, Dugast and Foucault (2020) present a model in which investors engage in costly and random search for predictor variables. Gabaix (2014) reexamines consumer theory and competitive equilibrium theory in a model in which attention to many variables is costly. Routledge (2019) studies an asset allocation problem in which investors have a preference for simplicity in the statistical model they use to inform their asset allocation decision.

It would be interesting to put such frictions into an asset pricing framework in which one can analyze questions about return predictability. Which types of data are more likely to be incorporated into prices; which types of data get ignored due to the frictions and then show up as predictable components in returns? Are there ways of calibrating these frictions to get quantitative predictions for the asset pricing consequences?

With a microfoundation for excessive sparsity or shrinkage, one could then also examine how these frictions changed over time and what consequences this had for asset prices. Investors several decades ago presumably found it much more costly to find, process, and analyze data.

Which features of the cash flow generating process are they therefore likely to have missed? How does this affect the return predictability that a current econometrician—armed with current data sets and computing power—may find in historical data from these earlier times?

6.3.2 Heterogeneity

Another stark simplification in the model outlined in Chapter 5 is the homogeneity of investors. All investors are identical and this is common knowledge. As a necessary consequence, investors' learning problem is limited to learning about exogenous fundamentals. Investors learn from realizations of exogenous cash flows about the properties of the cash flow process, but there is no scope for learning from endogenous variables and for learning about other market participants in this model.

Many interesting questions therefore remain unanswered. One has to do with heterogeneity in terms of sophistication. Some market participants have extremely strong data collection and analysis capabilities that help them to find profitable investment strategies in a high-dimensional environment. Other market participants may be less sophisticated and some of their investments decisions may be based on noise rather than signal. The trading of such noise traders in the marketplace may generate profitable opportunities for the sophisticated investors to exploit. But to do so, the sophisticated investors may need to learn from past price data about the behavior of the less sophisticated agents. Thus, introduction of heterogeneity in sophistication also introduces scope for learning from the endogenous price history. And in a high-dimensional environment where a large number of firm characteristics are relevant for predicting asset fundamentals, large numbers of these firm characteristics may also be relevant for teasing out from past price data the mispricings induced by noise trader demand. It would therefore be natural to model sophisticated investors as users of ML tools in their learning process.

Intuitively, many researchers would probably agree that there is a continuous process of mispricing discovery and elimination in financial markets, but there are very few formal models of this process. Moreover, for the learning about mispricing to be realistic in terms of its difficulty, this problem should be studied in a high-dimensional setting.

A recent paper by Davis (2020) takes some steps in this direction. In his model, ML investors use historical price data to learn about the mispricing induced by noise trader asset demand. In an early period, only noise traders are present. Through simulation, he examines to what extent mispricing gets eliminated in equilibrium when ML investors enter the market in future periods. Many interesting variations of this theme are still to be explored. For instance, what would be the optimal ML approach for the sophisticated investors in an environment like this? What would they do if they were Bayesians? Which prior beliefs would be objectively correct in this setting? If ML investors are present in multiple periods and continue to learn each period, does their learning problem get complicated by the fact that now past price data not only reflects noise trader activity but also the price impact of ML investors' own trading? What happens when capital available to ML investors depends on their past performance?

Given that there is a great deal of specialization among investors in financial markets, it would be interesting to examine heterogeneity among sophisticated investors. In reality, there seems to be a lot of sparsity in the models that professional investors use, explicitly or implicitly. For example, some focus on detailed fundamental analyses of a small number of companies, some conduct comprehensive statistical analyses in a broad cross-section of assets, others focus on signals embedded in assets' price histories. Each of these specialists omits a wide range of potentially predictive variables from their models.

To obtain such specialization and sparsity in a theoretical model, there has to be a cost associated with comprehensive, complex models. Moreover, investors have to be differentiated in some way. Heterogeneity in cost functions, for instance, could be a source of such differentiation. It would also be interesting to investigate whether slight random differences in initial conditions before investors approach data—say, in their prior beliefs, the data samples available to them, or the methods of analysis—in a high-dimensional environment could lead to substantial differences in their forecasting models.

It is an open question whether this specialization is important for equilibrium outcomes. Can one represent, at least approximately, the asset demands of such investors using sparse models with a representative investor who learns from public data, perhaps with shrinkage, but without imposing sparsity on the forecasting model? Or is something important getting lost in this approximation?

Balasubramanian and Yang (2020) is a recent example of a model of investor learning in a high-dimensional environment where heterogeneity is important for equilibrium outcomes. In their model, investors use publicly observed covariates to forecast fundamentals with a Bayesian regression along similar lines as in the model of Chapter 5. To form posterior beliefs, investors combine historical data with their prior beliefs about the model governing the asset fundamentals. While they all see the same public data, investors are heterogeneous in that they also receive private signals about fundamental value. In some sense, investors' models are extremely sparse because they only observe their own private signal, not the private signals of others. The key assumption in the model is that investors are uncertain about other investors' prior beliefs. If the environment is sufficiently high-dimensional, then, as a consequence of the uncertainty about others' priors, it can be near-optimal, in equilibrium, for investors to base their asset demands on their own statistical forecasts without conditioning on price. As a result, the equilibrium price contains more noise than it would if investors could frictionlessly share all information.

This model has some attractive features that push the modeling of investor learning toward greater realism: investors digest high-dimensional information, they specialize in different sources of information, they are sophisticated in their learning about asset fundamentals, and they are not sure about the priors others hold when they approach the data. What a model with heterogeneity of this kind would imply for in-sample and out-of-sample return predictability, and the evolution of this predictability over time, is still an open question.

In a multi-period setting, it could further be interesting to have some investors specialize in non-price predictors of asset fundamentals while others focus on information embedded in the price history. Such a theory would share similarities with Hong and Stein (1999)—a model that produces predictable under- and overreaction patterns in returns. In their model, fundamental information diffuses gradually and investors observing these signals do not condition their asset demands on price. Investors forecasting based on price history are able to use only a sparse representation of this price history. In their model, these assumptions are imposed ad hoc, but it would be interesting to examine whether a combination of a high-dimensional environment and uncertainty about other investors' priors could explain a neglect of conditioning on price and the sparsity of investors' models.

6.4   Concluding Remarks

Financial markets are places where participants process information from an incredibly rich array of data sources. ML methods allow researchers to bring this richness into empirical and theoretical studies of asset prices. As the earlier chapters in this book have demonstrated, embracing this richness leads to a novel perspective on asset prices. Empirical estimates of risk and return look different from what models with artificially imposed sparsity would suggest. The economic interpretation of these estimates in terms of risk premia, mispricing due to investor biases, or learning-induced return predictability is different as well.

There are exciting research opportunities at this frontier. Some new puzzles will emerge in empirical studies employing ML methods; others may find a resolution through theoretical models that account for the difficulty of investors' learning problem in high-dimensional environments. Altogether, this should lead to a better understanding of the dynamic process by which complex information is distilled into market prices.

BIBLIOGRAPHY

Amemiya, Takeshi, 1985. *Advanced Econometrics* (Harvard University Press, Cambridge, MA).

Angelosante, Daniele, and Georgios B. Giannakis, 2009, RLS-weighted lasso for adaptive estimation of sparse signals. In *2009 IEEE International Conference on Acoustics, Speech and Signal Processing*, pp. 3245–3248. IEEE.

Asness, Clifford S., Tobias J. Moskowitz, and Lasse H. Pedersen, 2013, Value and momentum everywhere, *Journal of Finance*, 929–985.

Athey, Susan, and Guido W. Imbens, 2019, Machine learning methods that economists should know about, *Annual Review of Economics* 11.

Athey, Susan, Julie Tibshirani, and Stefan Wager, 2019, Generalized random forests, *Annals of Statistics* 47, 1148–1178.

Avramov, Doron, Si Cheng, and Lior Metzker, 2019, Machine learning versus economic restrictions: Evidence from stock return predictability, Working paper, IDC Herzliyah.

Ba, Lei Jimmy, and Rich Caruana, 2013, Do deep nets really need to be deep?, Working paper, arXiv preprint arXiv:1312.6184.

Balasubramanian, Anirudha, and Yilin Yang, 2020, Statisticians' equilibrium: Trading with high-dimensional data, Working paper, Stanford University.

Barillas, Francisco, and Jay Shanken, 2018, Comparing asset pricing models, *Journal of Finance* 73, 715–754.

Bianchi, Francesco, Sydney C. Ludvigson, and Sai Ma, 2020, Belief distortions and macroeconomic fluctuations, Working paper, National Bureau of Economic Research.

Breiman, Leo, 2001, Random forests, *Machine Learning* 45, 5–32.

Breiman, L., J. H. Friedman, R. A. Olshen, and C. J. Stone, 1984. *Classification and regression trees* (Wadsworth, Belmont, CA).

Bryzgalova, Svetlana, Markus Pelger, and Jason Zhu, 2019, Forest through the trees: Building cross-sections of stock returns, Working paper, Stanford University.

Campbell, John Y., and Samuel B. Thompson, 2008, Predicting excess stock returns out of sample: Can anything beat the historical average?, *Review of Financial Studies* 21, 1509–1531.

Chan, Louis K. C., Jason Karceski, and Josef Lakonishok, 2003, The level and persistence of growth rates, *Journal of Finance* 58, 643–684.

Chen, Luyang, Markus Pelger, and Jason Zhu, 2019, Deep learning in asset pricing, Working paper, Stanford University.

Chinco, Alex, Adam D. Clark-Joseph, and Mao Ye, 2019, Sparse signals in the cross-section of returns, *Journal of Finance* 74, 449–492.

Chordia, Tarun, Amit Goyal, and Alessio Saretto, 2019, Anomalies and false rejections, *Review of Financial Studies* 33, 2134–2179.

Cochrane, John H., 2008, The dog that did not bark: A defense of return predictability, *Review of Financial Studies* 21, 1533–1575.

Cochrane, John H., 2011, Presidential address: Discount rates, *Journal of Finance* 66, 1047–1108.

Collin-Dufresne, Pierre, Michael Johannes, and Lars A. Lochstoer, 2017, Asset pricing when 'this time is different', *Review of Financial Studies* 30, 505–535.

Cybenko, George, 1989, Approximation by superpositions of a sigmoidal function, *Mathematics of Control, Signals and Systems* 2, 303–314.

Davis, Carter, 2020, Machine learning, quantitative portfolio choice, and mispricing, Working paper, University of Chicago.

DeBondt, Werner F. M., and Richard Thaler, 1985, Does the stock market overreact?, *Journal of Finance* 40, 793–805.

DeMiguel, Victor, Alberto Martin-Utrera, Francisco J Nogales, and Raman Uppal, 2019, A transaction-cost perspective on the multitude of firm characteristics, *Review of Financial Studies* 33, 2180–2222.

Dugast, Jérôme, and Thierry Foucault, 2020, Equilibrium data mining and data abundance, Working paper, HEC Paris.

Fama, Eugene F., 1970, Efficient capital markets: A review of theory and empirical work, *Journal of Finance* 25, 383–417.

Fama, Eugene F., and Kenneth R. French, 1993, Common risk factors in the returns on stocks and bonds, *Journal of Financial Economics* 33, 23–49.

Fama, Eugene F., and Kenneth R. French, 2008, Dissecting anomalies, *Journal of Finance* 63, 1653–1678.

Fama, Eugene F., and Kenneth R. French, 2015, A five-factor asset pricing model, *Journal of Financial Economics* 116, 1–22.

Fama, Eugene F., and Kenneth R. French, 2016, Dissecting anomalies with a five-factor model, *Review of Financial Studies* 29, 69–103.

Fan, Jianqing, Yuan Liao, and Weichen Wang, 2016, Projected principal component analysis in factor models, *Annals of Statistics* 44, 219.

Feng, Guanhao, Stefano Giglio, and Dacheng Xiu, 2020, Taming the factor zoo: A test of new factors, *Journal of Finance* 75, 1327–1370.

Feng, Guanhao, Nicholas G. Polson, and Jianeng Xu, 2018, Deep learning in characteristics-sorted factor models, *arXiv preprint arXiv:1805.01104*.

Freyberger, Joachim, Andreas Neuhierl, and Michael Weber, 2020, Dissecting characteristics nonparametrically, *Review of Financial Studies* 33, 2326–2377.

Gabaix, Xavier, 2014, A sparsity-based model of bounded rationality, *Quarterly Journal of Economics* 129, 1661–1710.

Gentzkow, Matthew, Bryan Kelly, and Matt Taddy, 2019, Text as data, *Journal of Economic Literature* 57, 535–74.

George, Edward I., and Dean P. Foster, 2000, Calibration and empirical Bayes variable selection, *Biometrika* 87, 731–747.

Gillen, Benjamin J., Sergio Montero, Hyungsik Roger Moon, and Matthew Shum, 2019, BLP-2LASSO for aggregate discrete choice models with rich covariates, *Econometrics Journal* 22, 262–281.

Gu, Shihao, Bryan Kelly, and Dacheng Xiu, 2020a, Empirical asset pricing via machine learning, *Review of Financial Studies* 33, 2223–2273.

Gu, Shihao, Bryan T. Kelly, and Dacheng Xiu, 2020b, Autoencoder asset pricing models, *Journal of Econometrics*, forthcoming.

Hamilton, James D., 1994. *Time Series Analysis* (Princeton University Press, Princeton, NJ).

Han, Yufeng, Ai He, David Rapach, and Guofu Zhou, 2019, Firm characteristics and expected stock returns, Working paper, Washington University.

Hansen, Peter Reinhard, and Allan Timmermann, 2015, Equivalence between out-of-sample forecast comparisons and Wald statistics, *Econometrica* 83, 2485–2505.

Harvey, Campbell R., Yan Liu, and Heqing Zhu, 2016, ... and the cross-section of expected returns, *Review of Financial Studies* 29, 5–68,

Hastie, Trevor, Robert Tibshirani, and Jerome Friedman, 2009. *The Elements of Statistical Learning* (2nd edition) (Springer, New York, NY).

Hastie, Trevor, Robert Tibshirani, and Martin Wainwright, 2015. *Statistical Learning with Sparsity: The Lasso and Generalizations* (CRC, Boca Raton, FL).

Heston, Steven L., and Ronnie Sadka, 2008, Seasonality in the cross-section of stock returns, *Journal of Financial Economics* 87, 418–445.

Hoerl, Arthur E., and Robert W. Kennard, 1970, Ridge regression: Biased estimation for nonorthogonal problems, *Technometrics* 12, 55–67.

Hong, Harrison, and Jeremy C Stein, 1999, A unified theory of underreaction, momentum trading, and overreaction in asset markets, *Journal of Finance* 54, 2143–2184.

Horel, Enguerrand, and Kay Giesecke, 2019, Towards explainable AI: Significance tests for neural networks, *arXiv preprint arXiv:1902.06021*.

Hornik, Kurt, Maxwell Stinchcombe, and Halbert White, 1989, Multilayer feed-forward networks are universal approximators, *Neural networks* 2, 359–366.

Hou, Kewei, Chen Xue, and Lu Zhang, 2015, Digesting anomalies: An investment approach, *Review of Financial Studies* 28, 650–705.

Inoue, Atsushi, and Lutz Kilian, 2005, In-sample or out-of-sample tests of predictability: Which one should we use?, *Econometric Reviews* 23, 371–402.

Jegadeesh, Narasimhan, and Sheridan Titman, 1993, Returns to buying winners and selling losers: Implications for market efficiency, *Journal of Finance* 48, 65–91.

Kelly, Bryan, Seth Pruitt, and Yinan Su, 2019, Characteristics are covariances: A unified model of risk and return, *Journal of Financial Economics* 134, 501–524.

Kogan, Leonid, and Mary Tian, 2015, Firm characteristics and empirical factor models: A model-mining experiment, Working paper, MIT.

Koijen, Ralph S. J., and Motohiro Yogo, 2019, A demand system approach to asset pricing, *Journal of Political Economy* 127, 1475–1515.

Kozak, Serhiy, 2019, Kernel trick for the cross section, Working paper, University of Maryland.

Kozak, Serhiy, Stefan Nagel, and Shrihari Santosh, 2018, Interpreting factor models, *Journal of Finance* 73, 1183–1223.

Kozak, Serhiy, Stefan Nagel, and Shrihari Santosh, 2020, Shrinking the cross-section, *Journal of Financial Economics* 135, 271–292.

LeCun, Yann, Yoshua Bengio, and Geoffrey Hinton, 2015, Deep learning, *Nature* 521, 436.

Lettau, Martin, and Markus Pelger, 2018, Factors that fit the time series and cross-section of stock returns, Working paper, National Bureau of Economic Research.

Lewellen, Jonathan, and Jay Shanken, 2002, Learning, asset-pricing tests and market efficiency, *Journal of Finance* 57, 1113–1145.

Lin, Henry W., Max Tegmark, and David Rolnick, 2017, Why does deep and cheap learning work so well?, *Journal of Statistical Physics* 168, 1223–1247.

Lindley, Dennis V., and Adrian F. M. Smith, 1972, Bayes estimates for the linear model, *Journal of the Royal Statistical Society: Series B (Methodological)* 34, 1–18.

Linnainmaa, Juhani T., and Michael R. Roberts, 2018, The history of the cross-section of stock returns, *Review of Financial Studies* 31, 2606–2649.

Lo, Andrew W., and A. Craig MacKinlay, 1990, Data-snooping biases in tests of financial asset pricing models, *Review of Financial Studies* 3, 431–467.

MacKinlay, A. Craig, 1995, Multifactor models do not explain deviations from the CAPM, *Journal of Financial Economics* 38, 3–28.

Martin, Ian, and Stefan Nagel, 2019, Market efficiency in the age of big data, Working paper, University of Chicago.

Martínez-Rego, David, Beatriz Pérez-Sánchez, Oscar Fontenla-Romero, and Amparo Alonso-Betanzos, 2011, A robust incremental learning method for non-stationary environments, *Neurocomputing* 74, 1800–1808.

McLean, David R., and Jeffrey Pontiff, 2016, Does academic research destroy stock return predictability?, *Journal of Finance* 71, 5–32.

Merton, R., 1980, On estimating the expected return on the market, *Journal of Financial Economics* 8, 323–361.

Molavi, Pooya, Alireza Tahbaz-Salehi, and Andrea Vedolin, 2020, Asset pricing with misspecified models, Working paper, Boston University.

Monti, Ricardo P., Christoforos Anagnostopoulos, and Giovanni Montana, 2018, Adaptive regularization for lasso models in the context of nonstationary data streams, *Statistical Analysis and Data Mining: The ASA Data Science Journal* 11, 237–247.

Moritz, Benjamin, and Tom Zimmermann, 2016, Tree-based conditional portfolio sorts: The relation between past and future stock returns, Working paper, University of Munich.

Nagel, Stefan, and Zhengyang Xu, 2019, Asset pricing with fading memory, Working paper, University of Chicago.

Novy-Marx, Robert, 2012, Is momentum really momentum?, *Journal of Financial Economics* 103, 429–453.

Novy-Marx, Robert, and Mihail Velikov, 2016, A taxonomy of anomalies and their trading costs, *Review of Financial Studies* 29, 104–147.

Pástor, L'uboš, and Robert F Stambaugh, 2000, Comparing asset pricing models: An investment perspective, *Journal of Financial Economics* 56, 335–381.

Ross, S. A., 1976, The arbitrage theory of capital asset pricing, *Journal of Economic Theory* 13, 341–360.

Routledge, Bryan R., 2019, Machine learning and asset allocation, *Financial Management* 48, 1069–1094.

Sims, Christopher A., 2003, Implications of rational inattention, *Journal of Monetary Economics* 50, 665 – 690.

Stone, Mervyn, 1977, An asymptotic equivalence of choice of model by cross-validation and Akaike's criterion, *Journal of the Royal Statistical Society: Series B (Methodological)* 39, 44–47.

Tibshirani, Robert, 1996, Regression shrinkage and selection via the lasso, *Journal of the Royal Statistical Society: Series B (Methodological)* 58, 267–288.

Tibshirani, Ryan J., and Robert Tibshirani, 2009, A bias correction for the minimum error rate in cross-validation, *Annals of Applied Statistics*, 822–829.

Timmermann, Allan G., 1993, How learning in financial markets generates excess volatility and predictability in stock prices, *Quarterly Journal of Economics*, 1135–1145.

Varma, Sudhir, and Richard Simon, 2006, Bias in error estimation when using cross-validation for model selection, *BMC Bioinformatics* 7, 91.

Wilson, D. Randall, and Tony R. Martinez, 1997, Bias and the probability of generalization. In *Proceedings Intelligent Information Systems. IIS'97*, pp. 108–114.

Wolpert, David H., 1996, The lack of a priori distinctions between learning algorithms, *Neural computation* 8, 1341–1390.

Zou, Hui, and Trevor Hastie, 2005, Regularization and variable selection via the elastic net, *Journal of the Royal Statistical Society: Series B (Statistical Methodology)* 67, 301–320.

INDEX